ABOUT THE AUTHORS

Gianfranco Conti taught for 25 years at schools in Italy, the UK and in Kuala L___, also been a university lecturer, holds a Master's degree in Applied Linguistics and a PhD in metacognitive strategies as applied to second language writing. He is now an author, a popular independent educational consultant and professional development provider. He has written around 2,000 resources for the TES website, which have awarded him the Best Resources Contributor in 2015. He has co-authored the best-selling and influential book for world languages teachers, "The Language Teacher Toolkit" and "Breaking the Sound Barrier: Teaching Learners how to Listen", in which he puts forth his Listening As Modelling methodology. Gianfranco writes an influential blog on second language acquisition called The Language Gym, co-founded the interactive website language-gym.com and the Facebook professional group Global Innovative Language Teachers (GILT). Last but not least, Gianfranco has created the instructional approach known as E.P.I. (Extensive Processing Instruction).

Dylan Viñales has taught for 15 years, in schools in Bath, Beijing and Kuala Lumpur in state, independent and international settings. He lives in Kuala Lumpur. He is fluent in five languages, and gets by in several more. Dylan is, besides a teacher, a professional development provider, specialising in E.P.I., metacognition, teaching languages through music (especially ukulele) and cognitive science. In the last five years, together with Dr Conti, he has driven the implementation of E.P.I. in one of the top international schools in the world: Garden International School. This has allowed him to test, on a daily basis, the sequences and activities included in this book with excellent results (his students have won language competitions both locally and internationally). He has designed an original Spanish curriculum, bespoke instructional materials, based on Reading and Listening as Modelling (RAM and LAM). Dylan co-founded the fastest growing professional development group for modern languages teachers on Facebook, Global Innovative Languages Teachers, which includes over 12,000 teachers from all corners of the globe. He authors an influential blog on modern language pedagogy in which he supports the teaching of languages through E.P.I. Dylan is the lead author of Spanish content on the Language Gym website and oversees the technological development of the site. He is currently undertaking the NPQML qualification, after which he plans to pursue a Masters in second language acquisition.

Ronan Jézéquel has taught for 15 years, in schools in Frimley, Brighton and Kuala Lumpur in state and international settings. He lives in Kuala Lumpur. He is fluent in three languages, and gets by in several more. Ronan is, besides a teacher, a keen mountain biker and an outdoor enthusiast. In the last five years, together with Dr Conti and Dylan Viñales, he has contributed to the implementation of E.P.I. in one of the top international schools in the world: Garden International School. This has allowed him to test, on a daily basis, the sequences and activities included in this book with excellent results. Ronan is the lead author of French content on The Language Gym website and he also brings the competitive element from his sporty background to TLG with the design of live games and features such as our leaderboard.

THE LANGUAGE GYM

ACKNOWLEDGEMENTS

Many thanks to the native speakers who contributed to the recording process. In particular, thanks to Julien Barrett, Sophie Barré, Alexia Barton, Julie Das and Sophie Youill for their time and effort in recording the sound files.

Secondly, our thanks and appreciation to the testing and proofreading team, Julien Barrett & Sophie Barré. It is thanks to their time, patience and professionalism that we have been able to produce a refined and highly accurate product.

FRENCH
SENTENCE BUILDERS

A lexicogrammar approach

Beginner to Pre-Intermediate

LISTENING
Student Book

Exercises and activities

 THE LANGUAGE GYM

Imprint: Independently Published

Edited by Julien Barrett

DEDICATION

For Catrina

- Gianfranco

For Ariella and Leonard

- Dylan

For Mariana

- Ronan

EXTENSIVE PROCESSING INSTRUCTION

If you have bought into our E.P.I. approach

Both this listening book and the original Sentence Builder book were originally designed as a resource to use in conjunction with our E.P.I. approach and teaching strategies. Our course favours flooding comprehensible input, organising content by communicative functions and related constructions, and a big focus on reading and listening as modelling. The aim of these books is to empower the beginner-to-pre-intermediate learner with linguistic tools - high-frequency structures and vocabulary - useful for real-life communication.

If you don't know or have NOT yet bought into our approach

If you would like to learn about E.P.I. you could read one of the authors' blogs. The definitive guide is Dr Conti's "Patterns First – How I Teach Lexicogrammar" which can be found on his blog (www.gianfrancoconti.com). There are also informative and user-friendly blogs on Dylan's Wordpress site (mrvinalesmfl.wordpress.com) such as "Using sentence builders to reduce (everyone's) workload and create more fluent linguists" which can be read to get teaching ideas and to learn how to structure a course, through all the stages of E.P.I.

The book "Breaking the Sound Barrier: Teaching Learners how to Listen" by Gianfranco Conti and Steve Smith, provides a detailed description of the approach and of the listening and speaking activities you can use in synergy with the present book.

INTRODUCTION

This French Listening Booklet matches to the minutest details the content of the 19 units included in the best-selling workbook for beginner-to-pre-intermediate learners "French sentence builders", by the same authors. For best results, the two books should be used together.

This book fully implements Dr Conti's popular approach to listening-skills instruction, L.A.M. (aka *Listening-As-Modelling*), laid out in his seminal work: "Breaking the Sound Barrier: Teaching Learners how to Listen" (Conti and Smith, 2019). L.A.M. is based on the concept that listening instruction should train students in the mastery of the key micro-listening skills identified by cognitive psychologists as follows:

- Phonemic processing
- Syllable processing
- Segmenting
- Lexical retrieval
- Parsing
- Meaning building
- Discourse building

This translates into aural instruction which deliberately targets the above micro-abilities through a range of tasks performed on input which is (1) highly patterned; (2) 90-98 % comprehensible; (3) flooded with the occurrence of the target structural patterns and lexical items; (4) delivered at a rate of speed which allows for learning; (5) designed to induce a priming effect on learning (i.e. to subconsciously sensitize the learners to the target language items).

Each unit contains around 13 listening tasks, which provide continuous and extensive recycling of the target constructions and vocabulary items and address the development of the key listening micro-skills. The tasks include engaging and tested Conti classics such as "Spot the intruder", "Missing details", "Faulty transcript", "Break the flow", "Faulty translation", "Gapped translation" and "Listening slalom", alongside more traditional listening comprehension tasks.

The tasks have been designed with the following key L.A.M. principles in mind: (1) the task's cognitive load must be appropriate to the level of the target learners; (2) the tasks must involve thorough processing (i.e. they should promote attention to details); (3) at the beginning stages, the tasks should promote noticing of the target language items by creating opportunities for cognitive comparison between the target language and the mother tongue (e.g. by using parallel texts in both languages, as happens in tasks such as "Bad translation" and "Gapped translation"); (4) the tasks should provide the learners with multiple entry points for acquisition by requiring them to engage with the same or similar texts at different levels of processing (from the identification of sounds to lexical retrieval; from the processing of structural patterns to the construction of meaning and discourse); (5) the tasks should model speaking micro-skills (e.g. pronunciation, decoding skills, functional and positional processing), not merely exam-taking techniques (as textbooks typically do); (6) tasks should be sequenced in a graded fashion, gradually phasing out support and increasing in difficulty.

The tasks have been tested countless times with students aged 11 to 13, with very positive feedback both in terms of engagement and perceived effectiveness. In particular, Dylan and Ronan have been pioneers of the approach and used it exclusively, and extensively, over the last 4 years at Garden International School, with excellent results in terms of both student engagement and progress.

HOW TO USE THIS BOOK

This book was intended as a Listening-for-learning tool aimed at paving the way for spoken and/or written production. If used in conjunction with the "French Sentence Builders" book, the tasks in each unit would follow the presentational stage of the target constructions through sentence builders and associated teacher-led aural activities aimed at building phonological awareness (e.g. "Faulty echo", "Minimal pairs", "Spot the silent letters", "Write it as you hear it") and at establishing meaning (e.g. "Listening bingo", "Positive or Negative", "Faulty transcript").

We recommend interspersing the listening tasks in each unit with engaging vocabulary-building, reading and read-aloud activities rather than covering every single exercise in a sequential fashion. Also, teachers, in selecting the activities and crafting each instructional sequence, should be cognizant of the motivational levels and concentration span of their students. These will vary from class to class and will inevitably inform their choice of the amount and type of listening that will be most conducive to learning.

Please note that whilst the sequence in which the tasks are arranged in each unit was carefully crafted by the authors to provide a graded and balanced progression from easier to more challenging, teachers should not feel straight-jacketed by that order.

If the teacher has near native or native command of the target language, they may want to deliver some of activities by reading the text aloud themselves using the transcripts provided in the accompanying teacher book (bought separately). This will enable them to enhance the input by emphasizing specific aspects of the input (e.g. specific words, word endings or phonotactic features such as assimilation phenomena) they may want their students to notice. Input enhancement is a useful means to enhance acquisition and interpersonal listening whereby the teacher interacts with the learners is an effective way to make aural input more learnable, engaging and motivational.

ACCESSING THE SOUND FILES

The sound files can be accessed at www.language-gym.com/listening (password is "**penguin**").

Once you log on, you will see a menu, containing all the units in the book, ordered and labelled as per the book itself.

IMPORTANT NOTICE: Please note, that this section of the Language Gym can be accessed by any person who has bought this book, regardless of whether or not you are a subscriber to the main Language Gym site. Under no circumstances should this password be shared with a teacher, **outside of your school**, who has not bought the book. This extends to other schools inside a collective of schools, such as a trust. In brief: every school should buy their own book. The book should not be shared outside of your school.

CHOOSING A DIFFICULTY LEVEL

Please note that several activities contain a normal and a "faster" version. These have been added in as a differentiation tool. It is up to the individual teacher's discretion which file to use, based on their knowledge of the students in their classes.

 THE LANGUAGE GYM

TABLE OF CONTENTS

UNIT 1 – TALKING ABOUT MY AGE

1. Complete the gaps

a. Je m' __ __ __ __ __ __ Alexandre.

b. J'ai __ __ __ __ __ ans.

c. J'ai __ __ __ __ frères.

d. __ __ __ frère aîné s'__ __ __ __ __ __ Robert.

e. Mon __ __ __ __ cadet __'appelle Julien.

f. Comment tu __'appelles?

g. Quel __ __ __ as-tu?

2. Break the flow

a. JemappelleAnthonyetjaidouzeans.

b. Jaiquinzeans.

c. MonfrèresappellePierre.

d. MasœursappelleAnne.

e. Quelâgeastu?

f. MonfrèresappellePhilippe.

g. Commenttutappelles?

3. Arrange in the order in which you hear

I am thirteen years old	
Anne is fifteen years old	
My name is Paul	
My sister is called Anne	
I have a brother and a sister	
My brother is called Fernand	
Fernand is seventeen years old	

4. Spot the differences and correct your text

a. Je m'appelle Karine.

b. J'ai onze ans.

c. J'ai deux sœurs.

d. Mon frère aîné s'appelle Marc.

e. Mon frère aîné s'appelle Robert.

f. Paul a quatorze ans.

g. Robert a huit ans.

h. Quel âge avez-vous?

5. Faulty translation: spot the nine translation errors and correct them

a. Her name is Émilie.

b. I am Québécoise.

c. I have three brothers.

d. My older sister is called Mélanie.

e. My younger sister is called Louise.

f. Mélanie is ten.

g. Léa is fourteen.

h. Me, I am eleven.

6. Spot and write in the seven missing words

a. Je m'appelle Pierre.

b. Je viens France.

c. J'ai treize.

d. J'ai un frère une sœur.

e. Mon frère appelle Robert.

f. Sœur s'appelle Isabelle.

g. Robert quatorze ans.

7. Spot and correct the errors in the text

a. J'a quatorze ans.

b. Je s'appelle Charles.

c. Mon frère s'appelle Pierre.

d. J'ai douze frères.

e. J'ai une frère et une sœur.

f. Quel âge est-il?

8. Listen and fill in the grid

		Age	Brothers	Sisters
1	Marie			
2	Joël			
2	Paul			
4	Anne			
5	Émilie			
6	Mélanie			

9. Complete with the missing letters

a. Je __'appelle Pierre.

b. Je suis d__ Pays basque.

c. J'ai quin__e ans.

d. Je n'ai p__s de frère.

e. Mais j'ai un__ sœur.

f. Ma soeur __'appelle Anne.

g. Alice a do__ze a__s.

h. Et toi, comment tu __appelles?

i. Quel âge as-t__?

10. Translate the nine sentences you hear into English

a.

b.

c.

d.

e.

f.

g.

h.

i.

11. Narrow listening one: gap-fill

Je m'appelle _____. Je suis de Quimper, en _____. Dans ma famille, il y a cinq personnes: _____ mère, mon père, mes _____ frères et moi. Mon frère _____ s'appelle Michel et mon frère _____ s'appelle Paul. Michel a _____ ans et mon frère Paul a _____ ans. Et toi, Comment tu t' _____? _____ âge as-tu?

appelles	Anthony	cadet	ma	six
aîné	quinze	France	quel	deux

12. Narrow listening two: gapped translation

My name is _____. I am from _____ in France. In my family there are _____ people: my mother, my father, my _____ brother, my _____ brother and myself. My _____brother is called _____. He is _____ years old. My _____ brother is called Anthony. He is _____ years old.

And you, what _____? How _____?

How_____?

UNIT 2 – SAYING WHEN MY BIRTHDAY IS

1. Complete

a. Je m'__ __ __ __ __ __ Alexandre et mon anniversaire est __ __ quinze __ __ __.

b. __ __ m'appelle Pierre et __ __ __ anniversaire __ __ __ le deux __ __ __ __.

c. Je m'appelle __ __ __ __ __ __ __ et mon anniversaire est __ __ trois __ __ __ __.

d. __ __ suis Léo et mon anniversaire est le __ __ __ __ __ __ __ __ __ __ __ __ __ __.

e. __ __ m'__ __ __ __ __ __ __ Paul et mon anniversaire __ __ __ le __ __ __ __ __ décembre.

2. Break the flow

a. Monanniversaireestletreizeoctobre.

b. Monanniversaireestleneufmai.

c. Quelleestladatedetonanniversaire?

d. Monanniversaireestlepremieraoût.

e. Monanniversaireestleseizejuillet.

f. Quelleestladatedesonanniversaire?

g. Monfrèreaquatorzeans.

h. Sonanniversaireestledeuxjanvier.

i. Quelleestladatedelanniversairedetonamie?

3. Arrange in the order in which you hear

Salut, je m'appelle Fernand.	
J'ai un frère.	
Je suis allemand.	
Son anniversaire est le cinq mars.	
Mais j'habite à Paris.	
J'ai dix ans.	
Mon anniversaire est le treize juillet.	

4. Spot the differences between the recording and the text: correct the sentences

a. Je m'appelle Julien.

b. Je n'ai pas de frères.

c. Je suis fille unique.

d. Je viens de la Réunion.

e. Mais j'habite en Italie.

f. J'ai quinze ans.

g. Mon anniversaire est le quatorze juin.

h. Ma petite amie Louise a treize ans.

i. Son anniversaire est le dix-huit octobre.

5. Faulty translation: spot the ten translation errors and correct them

a. My name is Robert and I am eleven years old. My birthday is on the 4th July.

b. My mother's name is Alice. She is 28 years old. Her birthday on the 13th August.

c. My father's name is Périg. He is 39 years old. His birthday is on the 10th January.

d. I have three brothers.

e. My brother Alex is 12 and his birthday is on the 2nd July.

f. My brother Nico is 9 and his birthday is on the 22nd May.

g. Do you have any brothers?

6. Spot and write in the nine missing details

Je m'appelle Robert, je suis français je vis en Allemagne. J'ai douze. Dans ma famille, il y a cinq: mon père, ma mère et deux frères. Mon frère aîné appelle Pierre et frère cadet s'appelle Romuald. Pierre a quinze ans et anniversaire est douze avril. Romuald a neuf ans et son anniversaire est vingt juillet.

7. Spot the errors in the sentences below: listen and correct

a. Mon anniversaire a le vingt juin.

b. Mon amie s'appelle Patricia. Il a dix ans et son anniversaire est le quinze mai.

c. L'anniversaire de mon amie est la neuf avril.

d. Ma mère avons trente-huit ans et son anniversary est le trente novembre.

e. Mon ami m'appelle Robert. Son anniversaire est le quatorze october.

8. Listen and fill in the grid

		Country	Age	Birthday
1	Alex			
2	Paul			
3	Nina			
4	Dylan			
5	Michel			
6	Martine			

9. Complete with the missing letters

a. Je m'appelle Ser__e.

b. Je n'ai pas de __rères.

c. Je suis fils __nique.

d. Je su__s du Portugal.

e. Mais j'h__bite en Italie.

f. J'ai quin__e ans.

g. Mon anniversaire est le quatorze __uin.

h. Ma pe__ite amie, Carmen, a treize ans.

i. Son anniversaire est le dix-hu__t octobre.

10. Translate the ten sentences you hear into English

a.

b.

c.

d.

e.

f.

g.

h.

i.

j.

11. Narrow listening one: gap-fill

Salut, je m'appelle Sylvie et je _____ de Biarritz, en France. J'ai _____ ans. Mon anniversaire est le _____ mai, j'ai deux frères, Philippe et Gérard. Philippe ___ quatorze ans et son anniversaire est le vingt-et-un _____. Mon frère Gérard a seize ans et _____ anniversaire est le _____ juin. À la _____ nous avons aussi un hamster. Il s'_____ Joli et a deux ans. Ma meilleure _____ s'appelle Magalie. Elle a _____ ans. Son anniversaire est le _____ janvier.

12. Narrow listening two: fill in the grid in English

Name	
Town	
Age	
Birthday	
Brother's age	
Brother's birthday	

13. Narrow listening three: gapped translation

My name is _____. I am _____ years old. I am from _____, in _____. My

birthday is on _____ _____. I have a _____ called _____. _____

is _____ years old. _____ birthday is on _____ _____. My best friend is called

_____. She is _____ years old and her birthday is on _____ _____. My

cousin is called _____. She is _____ years old and her birthday is on _____ _____. At

home we have a pet. It is a _____. Its name is _____ and it is _____ years old.

14. Listening slalom: write the correct numbers (#1 is done as an example)

1	2	3	4	5
My name is Andréa (1)	My brother is called Léon	My name is Alexandre	My name is Gabrièle	My name is Charles
I am from Valence	**I am from Calais (1)**	I am from Bayonne	He is from Saint-Étienne	I am from Grenoble
He is 14	I am 21	**I am 13 (1)**	I am 9	I am 16
His birthday is on 15th March	**My birthday is on 16th July (1)**	My birthday is on 21st May	My birthday is on 23rd June	My birthday is on 30th August
I have a girlfriend	I have a hamster	I have a boyfriend	He has a girlfriend	**I have a sister (1)**
His birthday is on 12th	Her birthday is on 7th	**Her birthday is on 1st (1)**	His birthday is on 2nd	Her birthday is on 30th
January (1)	March	October	June	September

15. Faulty translation: spot and correct the mistakes found in the translation

My name is Marc, I am from Italy. I am 13 years old. My parents are called Alain and Marina. They are 38

years old. My mother's birthday is on 21st March. My father's birthday is on 4th August. I have two sisters,

Raphaël and Anthony. Raphaël is 10 years old, and Anthony is 12. Raphaël's birthday is on 11th July.

Anthony's birthday in on 31st April. At home we have a pet, a snake. Its name is Pacotille, it's 1 year old.

I have a girlfriend. Her name is Patricia. She is 14. Her birthday is on 16th September.

UNIT 3 – DESCRIBING HAIR AND EYES

1. Complete

a. J'ai _ _ _ cheveux _ _ _ _.

b. Mon frère _ les cheveux _ _ _ _ _.

c. J'ai _ _ _ yeux _ _ _ _ _.

d. Anthony _ les _ _ _ _ _ _ _ blonds et les yeux _ _ _ _ _.

e. _ _ sœur _ _ _ _ _ des lunettes.

f. J'ai _ _ _ _ _ _ _ _ _ _ courts et en _ _ _ _.

g. J'ai les _ _ _ _ marron et _ _ _ une barbe.

2. Break the flow

a. Jailescheveuxnoirsetraides.

b. Iladegrandsyeuxbleus.

c. Ellealescheveuxnoirsetmi-longs.

d. Ilalescheveuxchâtainslongsetfrisés.

e. Jenaipasdecheveux.

f. Ellealesyeuxnoirsetelleportedeslunettes.

g. Tuaslesyeuxmarronettuasunemoustache.

3. Arrange in the order in which you hear

Je m'appelle François.	
J'ai douze ans.	
Mon anniversaire est le trente mars.	
J'ai les cheveux noirs, raides et courts.	
Je suis de Valence en France.	
Il a les cheveux blonds et les yeux verts.	
Il a quinze ans.	
Son anniversaire est le quatorze mars.	
J'ai un frère.	
J'ai les yeux noirs.	

4. Spot the intruders: identify the word in each sentence the speaker is not saying

a. J'ai les cheveux très longs.

b. Elle a les cheveux mi-longs.

c. Mon père a les cheveux assez courts.

d. Ma mère n'a pas les cheveux longs.

e. Mon frère cadet a les cheveux blonds.

f. Ma sœur a les cheveux noirs en épis.

5. Spot the differences between the recording and the text: correct the sentences

a. Je m'appelle Solène.

b. J'ai seize ans.

c. Je viens d'Angleterre.

d. …mais j'habite en Écosse.

e. J'ai les cheveux blonds et les yeux marron.

f. J'ai les cheveux longs et ondulés.

g. Ma meilleure amie, Catherine, a quatorze ans.

h. Elle est belle. Elle a les cheveux blonds, très longs et raides.

i. Elle a les yeux gris et elle porte des lunettes.

6. Complete

a. J'ai les cheveux en ép_ _ _ _ _ _.

b. J'ai les cheveux chât_ _ _ _ _ _.

c. J'ai les yeux no_ _ _ _ _ _.

d. J'ai les cheveux lo_ _ _ _ _ _.

e. J'ai les yeux bl_ _ _ _ _ _.

f. Je ne porte pas de lu_ _ _ _ _ _ _.

g. Je n'ai pas de mou_ _ _ _ _ _.

h. J'ai une bar_ _ _ _ _ _.

i. Mon père _ _ _ une moustache.

j. Mon frère a les yeux gr_ _ _ _ _.

7. Faulty translation: spot and correct the ten translation errors

a. My name is Charles. I am fourteen years old.

b. My birthday is on 14th June.

c. I have two brothers.

d. I have black hair, long and curly.

e. I have blue eyes and I wear glasses.

f. My older brother is called Paul. He is eighteen.

g. His birthday is on 20th July.

h. He has blond hair, short and wavy.

i. He has green eyes, and he wears glasses.

j. He has a moustache.

8. Spot the nine missing words and write them in

Je m'appelle Jean-Michel. J'ai cheveux blonds, longs frisés et les yeux bleus. Ma mère s'appelle Martine et mon père appelle Claude. Ma mère a les cheveux noirs, très longs et ondulés et yeux marron. Mon père est complètement et il a les yeux verts. J'ai un frère s'appelle Fernand. Il les cheveux blonds, courts et frisés et les yeux bleus. Fernand porte des lunettes. J'ai aussi une amie qui s'appelle Patricia. Elle a les cheveux roux, longs et raides. Elle a les yeux verts.

9. Spot the spelling/grammar errors in the sentences below: listen and correct

a. Je t'appelle Michel.

b. J'ai trois ans.

c. J'ai le cheveux noirs, longs et raides.

d. J'ai yeux bleus.

e. Je porte les lunettes.

f. Mon frère m'appelle Paul.

g. J'ai quatre ans.

h. Paul ai les cheveux blonds, courts et frisés.

i. Il a les yeux noirs. Il ne porte pas des lunettes.

10. Listen and fill in the grid

		Hair	Eyes	Wears glasses
1	Joël			
2	Paul			
3	Nina			
4	Dylan			
5	Michel			
6	Marie			

11. Translate the ten sentences you hear into English

a.   f.

b.   g.

c.   h.

d.   i.

e.   j.

12. Narrow listening three: gapped translation

My name is Véronique, I am _____ years old. My birthday is on the _____ of

_____. In my family there are _____ people: my father, my mother and my two

_____. My mother has _____ _____ hair, _____ and curly. She has

_____ eyes. My father has grey hair, _____ and straight. He has _____ eyes.

My two sisters have _____ hair, long and straight. They both have _____ eyes. I have

light brown, _____ _____ hair. However, before, I used to have _____ hair.

13. Listening slalom: write the correct numbers (#1 is done as an example)

1	2	3	4	5
My name is Marcel (1)	My name is Alice	My name is Magalie	My name is Kevin	My name is Jean-Claude
I am from Valence	**I am from Brussels (1)**	I am from Bayonne	I am from Saint-Étienne	I am from Grenoble
but I live in Rome, Italy	but I live in Paris	but I live in Dakar, Sénégal	**but I live in London, UK (1)**	but I live in Madrid, Spain
I have one brother	I have two brothers	**I am only child (1)**	I have one sister	I have one brother and one sister
I have blond hair	I have brown hair	I have red hair	I have black hair	**I have light brown hair (1)**
long and straight	short and spiky	**long and curly (1)**	short and wavy	medium length and straight
I have blue eyes (1)	I have brown eyes	I have green eyes	I have grey eyes	I have blue eyes

14. Fill in the grid

Name	Age	Birthday	Siblings	Hair (3 details)	Eyes
Matéo	12	13th August	one brother one sister	blond, short, curly	brown
Philippe		20th June		black, long, wavy	
André	16		two brothers		blue
Éric		8th March		brown, short, spiky	
Mélanie	11		one brother		brown
Alain		19th May		blond, short, curly	

UNIT 4 – SAYING WHERE I LIVE AND AM FROM

1. Fill in the blanks

(1) Salut. Je m'_____ David. J'habite dans une très grande _____ en centre-_____.

(2) Bonjour. Je m'appelle Chloé. Je _____ de Paris. Je _____ dans un petit appartement dans la _____.

(3) Comment ça va? Je ____ appelle Marie. Je suis ____ Calais. Je vis dans un joli _____ sur la côte.

(4) Salut. Je m'appelle _____. Je suis de Nouméa, en _____-_____. J'habite dans une très _____ maison à la montagne.

(5) _____. Je m'appelle Daniel, j'habite à Bruxelles, en _____. Je vis dans un bâtiment _____ dans le centre de Bruxelles.

(6) _____. Je m'appelle Béatrice. J'habite dans _____ grande maison, mais elle est un peu _____.

2. Multiple choice quiz: select the correct location

	a	b	c
Xavier	Brest	Valence	Grenoble
Samuel	Calais	Mende	Laval
Jean-Paul	Limoges	Sarlat	Lyon
Pascal	Toulouse	Quimper	Marmande
Céline	Brest	Biarritz	Paris
Aurélie	Bordeaux	Dijon	Marseille
Gabrièle	Saint-Tropez	Quimper	Nice
Patrice	Limoges	Marmande	Saint-Etienne
Emmanuel	Rennes	Mulhouse	Biarritz

3. Spot the intruders: identify the words the speaker is NOT saying

Salut. Je m'appelle Julien. J'ai âge quatorze ans et j'habite dans à Dakar, le la capitale du Sénégal. Dans ma famille, nous sommes il y a quatre personnes: mes parents, ma sœur, mon frère et moi. Mon frère qui s'appelle Benjamin. J'habite dans une la petite maison dans le centre de Dakar. Ma maison est très jolie.

4. Geographical mistakes: listen and correct

(1) Je m'appelle Nina. Je suis de Brest. Brest est en Dordogne.

(2) Je m'appelle Pierre. Je suis de Dakar. Dakar est au Portugal.

(3) Je m'appelle Clémence. Je suis de Libreville. Libreville est à Madagascar.

(4) Je m'appelle Jean. Je suis de Montréal. Montréal est au Mali.

(5) Je m'appelle Julie. Je suis de Casablanca. Casablanca est au Canada.

(6) Je m'appelle Aurélie. Je suis de Nice. Nice est en Alsace.

5. Spelling challenge: which city names are being spelled out? Fill in the grid

1	
2	
3	
4	
5	
6	
7	

6. Faulty translation: spot and correct the translation errors

My name is Marie. I am from Guadeloupe, but I live in France. I am twelve. I live in Brittany, a region in the northeast of France.

I have blond hair and blue eyes. My hair is long and curly.

I live in a small flat in the centre of Rennes, with my mother Éliane and my two brothers, Sylvie and Pauline.

My flat is in an old building. It is pretty.

My father lives in a small house on the outskirts. His house is ugly and modern.

7. Spot the missing words and write them in

(1) J'habite Nouméa, la capitale la Nouvelle Calédonie. Nouméa est une belle ville. Je vis dans un appartement dans un bâtiment moderne centre-ville.

(2) J'habite avec ma famille à Cannes, une ville touristique dans le sud la France. Je vis dans maison moderne dans la banlieue de ville.

(3) J'habite à Saint-Denis, la capitale de La Réunion. Je vis avec ma famille et chien. J'habite dans un grand appartement, il est moche et dans un bâtiment.

(4) Je vis à Valence, France. J'habite une grande maison moderne sur la côte.

8. Complete the grid, as shown in the example (names are spelt out for you)

Name	Country	Type of accommodation	House/flat location	Two details about the house/flat
1. Anne	France	House	Town centre	1. Ugly 2. Big

 **THE LANGUAGE GYM**

9. Narrow listening: gapped translation

My name is Julien. I am _____ years old and my birthday is on _____ August. I _____ in Biarritz, in the Basque country, in the _____ of France. I live in an _____ house on the _____. I have two _____, Marie and Sylvie. Marie is very _____, but a bit silly. Sylvie is a bit _____, but very _____ and funny. My friend Romain _____ in Bordeaux, but he is from Biarritz like _____. He lives in a modern _____ in the _____. He has a big dog called _____. He lives in a big and _____ flat.

10. Listening slalom: follow the speaker from top to bottom and number the boxes accordingly

1	2	3	4	5
I live in Gabon, (1)	I am from Switzerland and	I am from Belgium and	I am from Morocco and	I am from France and
I live in Marrakesh.	I live in Brussels.	I live near Geneva.	I live in Cannes.	**near Libreville. (1)**
I am 12 and	**I am 15 and (1)**	I am 14 and	I am 16 and	I am 13 and
I live in a big house	I live in a small house	I live in a very small house	**I live in a small flat (1)**	I live in a flat
in a modern building. (1)	in an old building.	in the city centre.	near a lake.	on the coast.
I like my house	**My flat is ugly (1)**	My house	My flat is cosy	My house is pretty
and beautiful.	and spacious.	**but very big. (1)**	is modern.	because it is big.

11. Narrow listening: fill in the grid as shown in the example (Matéo)

Name	Age	Birthday	Town	Accommodation	Description	Location
Matéo	*14*	*20th May*	*Marseille*	*House*	*Big*	*Coast*
Philippe						
André						
Éric						
Mélanie						
Pauline						

THE LANGUAGE GYM

UNIT 5 – TALKING ABOUT MY FAMILY MEMBERS (AGE & RELATIONSHIPS)

1. Fill in the blanks

a. Dans ma _ _ _ _ _ _ _ , il y a _ _ _ _ personnes.

b. Mon grand-père a _ _ _ _ _ _ _ _ _ _-_ _ ans.

c. Dans _ _ famille, _ _ _ _ six _ _ _ _ _ _ _ _.

d. Mon _ _ _ _ s'appelle _ _ _ _ _ _.

e. Je m'_ _ _ _ _ _ _ bien avec _ _ _ frère _ _ _ _.

f. Je m'entends _ _ _ avec ma _ _ _ _.

g. Je m'entends _ _ _ _ bien avec mon _ _ _ _.

2. Break the flow

a. Ilyaquatrepersonnesdansmafamille.

b. Jementendsbienavecmesparents.

c. Mongrand-pèreaquatre-vingtsans.

d. Mononcleaquaranteans.

e. Monfrèreaînésappelle Jean.

f. Dansmafamilleilyacinqpersonnes.

g. Monpèreaquarante-deuxans.

3. Multiple choice quiz: select the correct age

		a	b	c
1	Julien	40	50	60
2	Sylvie	90	80	70
3	Jean	30	40	60
4	Pierre	60	70	100
5	Marina	36	46	56
6	Clémence	65	85	95
7	Éric	33	63	73
8	Paul	71	21	41
9	Émma	57	67	47

4. Spot the intruders: identify the word(s) in each sentence the speaker is NOT saying

a. Dans ma famille, il y a cinq mille personnes.

b. Mon oncle Pierre a quarante-et-un ans.

c. Je m'entends très bien avec mes parents.

d. Mon cousin Tristan a comme cinquante ans.

e. Mes grands-parents maternels ont quatre-vingts ans.

f. Je m'entends mal avec mon cousin Jean.

5. Listen, spot and correct the errors

a. Mon grand-père a quatre-vingt-deux ans.

b. Il y a cinq personnes dans ma famille.

c. Dans ma famille, il y a six personnes: ma mère, mon beau-père et mes trois frères.

d. Quel âge a ta sœur cadette?

e. Mon oncle a soixante-dix ans.

f. Je m'entends bien avec mes parents, surtout avec ma mère.

g. Dans ma famille, il y a quatre personnes.

6. Complete the words then write the number it refers to.

a. (Exemple) **Quatre-vingt-sept (87)**

b. Quatre-_ _ _ _ _-quinze

c. Vingt-_ _ _ _

d. _ _ _rante-trois

e. _ _nt

f. Quatre-vingt-_ _ _-huit

g. Cin_ _ _ _ _ _-neuf

h. Soixante-_ _ _ _ _ _ _ _

7. Faulty translation: spot the translation errors and correct them

a. My name is Jean-François. I am 16 years old.

b. I have blond and long hair.

c. I have green eyes.

d. In my family there are 4 people: my father, my mother, my cousin, my brother and me.

e. My father is 54, my mother is 34, my sister is 9 and my brother is 7.

f. My uncle and my aunt are called Robert and Martine. My uncle is 70 and my aunt is 51 years old.

g. My maternal grandparents are 80 years old.

h. My paternal grandfather is 76.

8. Spot and write in the missing words

a. Je appelle Dylan.

b. Je viens Espagne.

c. J'ai frère.

d. Mon anniversaire le vingt mars.

e. Dans ma famille, nous cinq personnes.

f. Il y a mon père, ma mère, mes frères et moi.

g. J'ai trente ans. Ma mère a soixante-deux ans et mon père a soixante ans.

h. Mon frère a quarante ans et mon frère a trente-cinq ans.

i. Je m'entends bien mes parents.

9. Listen, spot and correct the errors

a. Je s'appelle Raphaël.

b. Je suis quinze ans.

c. Mon anniversaire le treize mai.

d. Dans ma famille, est quatre personnes: mes parents, mon frère aîné et je.

e. Mon père est quarante ans.

f. Ma mère a quarante-douze ans.

g. Mon frère aîné a vingtun ans.

h. Entends bien avec mes parents.

i. Je m'entends mal en mon frère.

10. Fill in the table with the following names and add the missing ages:

~~Alex~~	Nina	Marie	Dylan	Paul	Michel

	Names	Father's age	Mother's age	Sibling's age
1	Alex	56	48	18
2		43		15
3			51	
4		55		17
5			68	
6			47	10

11. Translate the ten sentences you hear into English

a.

b.

c.

d.

e.

f.

g.

h.

i.

j.

12. Narrow listening: gapped translation

My name is Paul. I am from _____. I am _____ years old. My birthday is on

_____ _____. I have _____, long and _____ hair. I have

_____ eyes. In my family there are _____ people: my _____, my mother

and my two sisters. My older sister is _____ years old. My younger sister is _____

years old. I _____ with my parents. My _____ grandfather lives with us.

He is _____ years old. I get along with him.

13. Listening slalom: follow the speaker from top to bottom and number the boxes accordingly

1	2	3	4	5
Name: Hélène (1)	Name: Philippe	Name: Marie	Name: Xavier	Name: Jean
I am 17	**I am 16 (1)**	I am 20	I am 11	I am 30
My birthday is on 25 October	My birthday is on 20 June	**My birthday is on 31 December (1)**	My birthday is on 15 March	My birthday is on 7 January
My mother is 50	**My mother is 48 (1)**	My mother is 44	My mother is 39	My mother is 62
My father is 49	My father is 43	My father is 53	My father is 64	**My father is 52 (1)**
My grandad is 81	My grandad is 75	**My grandad is 76 (1)**	My grandad is 73	My grandad is 90
My grandma is 68 (1)	My grandma is 80	My grandma is 81	My grandma is 72	My grandma is 79

14. Narrow listening: listen and fill in the missing details on the grid

Name	Age	Birthday	Family size	<u>Older</u> sibling's age	Mother's age	Father's age
Andréa		20 June		16		41
Philippe	14		5			44
Sophie		15 Sept			43	
Éric	13		5		39	
Myriam	28			31		55

UNIT 6 – DESCRIBING MYSELF AND ANOTHER FAMILY MEMBER

1. Multiple choice quiz: select the correct adjective for each sentence

		a	b	c
1	My father is…	generous	fun	muscular
2	My mother is…	fat	intelligent	thin
3	My older sister is…	stupid	tall	muscular
4	My younger sister is…	tall	short	pretty
5	My brother is…	friendly	unfriendly	ugly
6	My cousin Paul is…	big	strong	small
7	My cousin Marie is…	lazy	bad	boring
8	My grandfather is…	mean	stubborn	annoying
9	My grandmother is...	generous	nice	fun
10	My girlfriend is…	patient	fat	muscular

2. Split sentences: listen and match

1. Didier		Fun
2. Sylvie		Boring
3. Morgan		Short
4. Kevin		Tall
5. Marine		Good-looking
6. Ariane		**Mean (1)**
7. Éric		Muscular
8. Paul		Ugly
9. Adeline		Stubborn
10. Manu		Strong

3. Spot the intruders: identify the word in each sentence the speaker is NOT saying

a. Mon frère est très beau.

b. Mon oncle Paul a quarante ans. Il est assez marrant.

c. Je m'entends très bien avec mon père parce qu'il est assez généreux.

d. Mon cousin Yann n'est pas très grand.

e. Ma sœur est de la taille moyenne.

f. Ma petite amie est trop bavarde.

4. Spot the differences and correct your text

a. Ma grand-mère est très patiente.

b. Ma mère est très intelligente.

c. Dans ma famille, il y a cinq personnes: ma mère, mon père, mes deux frères et moi.

d. Comment vas-tu?

e. Mon oncle a soixante ans, mais il est très ennuyeux.

f. Je m'entends mal avec mes parents, surtout avec ma mère car elle est très antipathique.

g. Dans ma famille, nous sommes tous petits.

5. Categories: listen to the words below and classify them in positive and negative

ADJECTIFS POSITIFS	ADJECTIFS NÉGATIFS

6. Faulty translation: spot and correct the translation errors

a. My name is Jean Paul. I am 16 years old. I have black hair and green eyes. I am tall, muscular and quite good-looking. I am friendly, talkative and quite generous.

b. My mother is called Patricia. She is fifty years old. She is short, slim and very ugly. She is generous, but a bit lazy.

c. My father is called Robert. He is 62 years old. He is neither tall nor short. He is quite handsome. He is very generous, strict and patient.

d. My sister is called Carla. She is 17. She is quite tall and slim. She is unfriendly and boring. She is also quite stubborn and lazy.

8. Listen and complete with the correct masculine or feminine ending

a. Elle est très **grand_**.

b. Ils sont très **méchant_**.

c. Ma mère et mon père sont très **paresseu_**.

d. Je suis **petit_** et **patient_**.

e. Tu es si **amusan_** !

f. Elles sont **méchant_ _** !

g. Leurs **fi _ _ _ _** sont très **gros _ _ _**.

h. Mes **fi_ _** sont très **travailleur_**.

i. Tu es si **marrant_** !

7. Spot the missing words and write them in

a. Je m'appelle David et très travailleur.

b. Mon frère est paresseux.

c. Ma mère est têtue antipathique.

d. Mon frère est de moyenne.

e. Mes parents très timides.

f. Ma sœur est très généreuse.

g. Je déteste cousin, car il est têtu.

9. Listen and fill in the grid

	Person	Description
1	My father is	
2	My mother is	
3	My sister is	
4	My brother is	
5	My cousin Paul is	
6	My cousin Marie is	
7	My grandfather is	
8	My grandmother is	
9	My best friend is	

10. Translate the ten sentences you hear into English

1.   6.

2.   7.

3.   8.

4.   9.

5.   10.

11. Narrow listening: gapped translation

My name is Paul. I love my parents. They are a bit _____, but very generous, _____ and hard-working. I have _____ brothers and one sister. My older brother is very annoying: he is _____, lazy, _____, _____ and too talkative. My younger brother is charming: he is nice, _____, patient, _____, and hard-working. My sister is very pretty and _____, but very boring. I also have a _____. Her name is Pauline. She is tall, _____, pretty and she is also very _____.

12. Listening slalom: follow the speaker from top to bottom and number the boxes accordingly

1	2	3	4	5
My name is Naomi (1)	My name is Anne	My name is Manuela	My name is Kevin	My name is Jean-Charles
I am 15 years old	**I am 17 years old (1)**	I am 18 years old	I am 13 years old	I am 12 years old
I am tall and fat	I am neither tall nor short	**I am tall and slim (1)**	I am not very tall	I am short and slim
My older brother is short and slim	My older sister is short and slim	My younger brother is short and slim	My older sister is short and very pretty	**My younger brother is tall and strong (1)**
I like her	I get along well with him	I like her a lot	**I get along well with him (1)**	I don't get along with him
because he is likeable and positive	because she is generous	because he is mean	because she is fun	**because he is patient and helpful. (1)**
and likeable.	Furthermore, he is very funny.	**He is also very generous and kind. (1)**	and funny.	and stubborn.

13. Narrow listening: fill in the grid

Name	Name of older sibling	Age of older sibling	Birthday of older sibling	Character of older sibling	Appearance of older sibling
Philippe					
Andréa					
Éric					
Mélanie					

 **THE LANGUAGE GYM**

1. Multiple choice quiz

		a	b	c
1	At home we have…	four pets	two pets	five pets
2	I have a…	turtle	dog	cat
3	My brother has a…	turtle	fish	parrot
4	My older sister has a…	lizard	rabbit	duck
5	My younger sister has a…	mouse	fish	horse
6	My mother has a…	cat	dog	parrot
7	My father has a…	bird	horse	dog
8	My grandparents have two…	dogs	horses	rabbits
9	My best friend has a…	lizard	dog	snake
10	My girlfriend has a…	fish	cat	dog

2. Split sentences: listen and match

1. Alexandra	a. A dog
2. Sylvie	b. A rabbit
3. Carmen	c. A parrot
4. Jean	d. A fish
5. Fabrice	e. A cat
6. Pascal	f. A horse
7. Jules	g. Two dogs
8. Véronique	h. Two turtles
9. Robert	i. Two mice
10. Simone	j. A mouse

3. Spot the intruders: identify the word in each sentence the speaker is not saying

a. Mon frère a un grand chien.

b. Ma meilleure amie n'a pas deux animaux.

c. Mes grands-parents ont deux petits chevaux.

d. La tortue verte de mon frère s'appelle Kura.

e. Ma petite amie a un chat blanc.

f. Mon chien marron est mignon, mais un peu paresseux.

g. J'ai deux poissons orange.

4. Spot the differences and correct your text

a. Mon chien est très mignon.

b. Mon chat est très intelligent.

c. Nous avons quatre animaux: un chien, un chat, un perroquet et un poisson rouge.

d. Tu as un hamster?

e. Mon oncle a une souris et un serpent chez lui.

f. Ma sœur a un cochon d'Inde très moche.

g. Nous avons deux chiens et un cheval chez nous.

h. Paul a un très grand rat noir chez lui!

5. Categories: listen to the sentences and write in any adjectives or nouns you hear into the table

	NOMS (Nouns)	ADJECTIFS (Adjectives)
1		
2		
3		
4		
5		
6		
7		
8		

6. Spot the missing words and write them in

Je m'appelle Jean. J'ai animaux: un chien s'appelle Rufus, un chat qui appelle Tarzan et serpent qui s'appelle Boa. Rufus trois ans. Il est noir et blanc. Il est gros et tranquille. Tarzan est tigré et distant. Il a grands yeux verts. Il est intelligent, mais ennuyeux. Il a quatre ans. Boa est un très grand serpent. Il a un an.

7. Fill in the blanks

Chez moi, nous avons trois _____ : un chien, un _____ et un _____. Mon chien s'_____ Bandit. Il est _____. Je l'aime parce qu'il est _____ et _____. Mon lapin s'appelle Zorro. Il est _____ et _____. Il est très _____ et _____. Mon rat s'appelle Rico. Il est _____ et blanc. Il est très intelligent et _____. Je l'_____.

8. Faulty translation: correct the translation

My name is Robert I am fifteen years old and I live in Marseille. In my family there are three people: my parents, my older brother, Jean, and myself. Jean is twelve years old and he is very boring. We have three pets: a parrot who is called Léo, a cat who is called Bingo and a lizard who is called Casper. Léo is very talkative. Bingo is skinny and Casper is boring, like my brother.

9. Listen and fill in the grid

Family member	Description
1. My father is	
2. My mother is	
3. My sister is	
4. My brother is	
5. My cousin Paul is	
6. My cousin Marie is	
7. My grandad is	
8. My grandma is	

10. Translate the ten sentences you hear into English

1.
2.
3.
4.
5.
6.
7.
8.
9.
10.

11. Sentence puzzle: rewrite correctly

a. J'ai un gris rat, un très lapin blanc et chat un marron.

b. Chat mon s'appelle Grassouillet parce qu'il beaucoup mange.

c. Mon Paul ami a un très serpent grand, noir et vert Venin qui s'appelle.

d. Nous avons une verte tortue Caroline qui s'appelle et une marron souris s'appelle qui Mascotte.

12. Narrow listening: gapped translation

My name is Patricia. I am _____ years old and _____ in London. In my family there are

_____ people: my _____, my mother, my _____ brother, my _____ and me.

We have a few _____. Firstly, we have a _____dog called Maximus. He is _____ and

beautiful. He is very _____ and eats _____. We also have a _____ called Leonardo. My

turtle is small, green and _____. She is very quiet. Finally, we have a _____ called Charlie. He

is very _____ and cute. He is red, _____ and _____. I love my pets.

13. Listening slalom: follow the speaker from top to bottom and number the boxes accordingly

1	2	3	4	5
We have three (1)	I have	My friend has	My grandparents have	My friend has
four pets at home.	**pets at home. (1)**	five pets at home.	six pets at home.	one pet at home:
A blue fish,	Two big black dogs,	**A green turtle, (1)**	a big fat cat.	Three fat, white guinea pigs,
He is black and white.	a big brown dog	a beautiful yellow bird,	**very slow and funny, (1)**	a yellow parrot
which is talkative and funny	**a cute and fat dog (1)**	a very fat duck	a cute guinea pig and	He is very lazy
and boring.	and a very cute black rabbit.	**and a goldfish. (1)**	a fun white mouse.	and two pretty Siamese cats.

14. Narrow listening: fill in the grid

Name	Age	Appearance	Character	Type of pet	Pet description (3 details)
1. Jean-Michel					
2. Mariane					
3. Pierre					
4. Hélène					

1. Multiple choice quiz: select the correct job

	1	2	3
Élise	accountant	nurse	housewife
Rose	lawyer	farmer	mechanic
Pascal	engineer	businessman	doctor
Paul	househusband	singer	cook
Anne	waitress	receptionist	housewife
Alice	farmer	actress	doctor
Martine	teacher	astronaut	postman
Samuel	lawyer	worker	mechanic
Léon	policeman	singer	cook
Léa	student	doctor	farmer

2. Listening for detail: did you hear the masculine or the feminine form? Circle the correct answer

MASCULINE	FEMININE
acteur	actrice
cuisinier	cuisinière
homme d'affaires	femme d'affaires
fermier	fermière
travailleur	travailleuse
avocat	avocate
ennuyeux	ennuyeuse
actif	active
marrant	marrante

3. Split sentences: listen and match

1. Yvan	a. worker
2. Sylvie	b. lawyer
3. Paul	c. doctor
4. Philippe	d. cook
5. Caroline	e. accountant
6. Jean	f. hairdresser
7. Véronique	g. teacher
8. Jules	h. mechanic
9. Robert	i. footballer
10. Marie	**j. actor (1)**

4. Spot the intruders

Je m'appelle Jean-Marc et je vais parler de ma famille. Dans ma famille, nous sommes trois personnes: mon père, ma mère, mon frère et moi. Mon père s'appelle Pascal. Il a cinquante-six ans. Il est très grand et un peu gros. Il est chauve. Il est sympathique et aussi travailleur. Il travaille comme un comptable. Il n'aime pas cela, car c'est un travail bien payé. Ma mère travaille comme une coiffeuse. Elle adore ça travail car lui c'est très amusant et gratifiant. Moi, je voudrais travailler comme un cuisinier et être connu comme Gordon Ramsay.

5. Listen, spot and correct the errors

Je m'appelle Marin. Je suis de Biarritz. Ma personne préférée dans ma famille, c'est ma mère. Elle est timide, mais très sympathique. Ma mère est comptable, mais maintenant elle ne travaille pas. Je déteste mon père. Il est intelligent, mais très antipathique. Mon père est mécanicien, mais il déteste son travail car c'est difficile et ennuyeux. Il travaille dans un garage à Biarritz. Chez moi, j'ai une souris qui s'appelle Donatello. Elle est lente mais très gentille, comme ma sœur Cassandra.

6. Categories: listen to the sentences and classify the words (in French)

NOMS (Nouns)	ADJECTIFS (Adjectives)
1.	
2.	
3.	
4.	
5.	
6.	

7. Spot the missing words and write them in

Je m'appelle Marie. Dans ma famille quatre personnes. Mon père s'appelle Émilien et avocat. Aime son travail, car c'est stimulant. Cependant, c'est stressant. Ma mère est femme foyer et elle aime assez travail. Elle dit c'est très gratifiant. Chez moi, j'ai un chien s'appelle Calin. Il est très amusant! Il n'aime pas les chats.

8. Faulty translation: correct the errors

My name is Philippe. I am twenty years old and live in Casablanca, in Morocco. In my family, there are four persons. I have a very funny dog called Jeannot. My father works as a cook in a restaurant in the town centre. He doesn't like his job because it's stressful. My mother is a doctor. She likes a lot her job because it's rewarding and easy.

9. Listen and fill in the grid

Person	Job
1. My father	
2. My mother	
3. My older brother	
4. My younger brother	
5. My sister	
6. My best friend	
7. My girlfriend	
8. My grandfather	

10. Translate the sentences into English

1.

2.

3.

4.

5.

6.

7.

8.

9.

11. Listen, spot and correct the errors

a. Je travaillez à la campagne.

b. Ma mère travaillons comme cuisinière.

c. Mon père a coiffeur.

d. Mes frères ne travaillent plus.

e. Ma petite amie est acteur.

f. Mon meilleur ami est pompière.

g. Ma cousin est médecin.

h. Mes oncles est fermiers.

12. Narrow listening: gapped translation

My name is _____. In my family there are _____ people. My _____ is

called Christian. He is tall and _____. He works as a _____. He loves his

job because it is _____. My mother is an _____. She does not _____ her

job because it is _____. She wants to be a _____ because it is _____and

she is very _____. My two _____ are students at _____. They love it

because it is _____ and _____. I am still a _____ in a secondary school.

I hate school because it is _____ and _____.

13. Listening Comprehension: listen and answer the questions about Valérie and Fernand

TEXT 1: Valérie		TEXT 2: Fernand	
Her father's job:		What job does his father do?	
What does he think about his job?		What does he think about his job?	
What job does her mother do?		What job does his mother do?	
What does she think about her job?		What does she think about her job?	
What job does Valérie want to do one day?		What job does Fernand want to do one day?	
Why?		Why?	

14. Fill in the grid

Name	Age	Character and appearance	Father's job	Mother's job	His/her ideal job
Jean-Marc					
Marie					
Pierre					
Andréa					

THE LANGUAGE GYM

UNIT 9 – COMPARING PEOPLE'S APPEARANCE AND PERSONALITY

1. Multiple choice quiz: select the correct adjective

	1	2	3
Alex	boring	tall	friendly
Rose	short	unfriendly	young
Pascal	hard-working	noisy	relaxed
Paul	fat	slim	good-looking
Amélie	strong	lazy	stupid
Pierre	short	unfriendly	young
Marie	strong	fat	stupid
Steven	slim	lazy	friendly
Tristan	strong	sporty	serious
Léa	hard-working	noisy	lazy

2. Listening for detail: did you hear the masculine or the feminine form?

MASCULINE	FEMININE
ennuyeux	ennuyeuse
bavard	bavarde
paresseux	paresseuse
bruyant	bruyante
généreux	généreuse
grand	grande
sportif	sportive
sérieux	sérieuse
travailleur	travailleuse
amusant	amusante

3. Complete with 'plus…que', 'moins…que' or 'aussi…que' as shown in the example

a. (exemple) *Ma mère est plus grande que mon père.*

b. Mon frère est _____ sportif _____ moi.

c. Mon chat est _____ paresseux _____ mon chien.

d. Je suis _____ fort _____ mon cousin.

e. Mon oncle est _____ vieux _____ mon grand-père.

f. Mon meilleur ami est _____ petit _____ moi.

g. Mon oncle est _____ gros _____ mon père.

h. Ma cousine Julie est _____ belle ____ ma cousine Léa.

4. Listen and fill in the middle column as shown in the example with the missing information in English

Anne	*is taller than*	*Philippe*
Sylvie		**Alain**
Jean		**Pierre**
Paul		**Jules**
Marie		**Gérard**
Caroline		**Léa**
Julien		**Julie**
Philippe		**Léon**
Dylan		**Samuel**
Véronique		**Serge**

5. Spot the differences and correct your text

a. Je suis plus grand que ma mère.

b. Mon cousin est aussi paresseux que moi.

c. Mon meilleur ami est plus bavard que moi.

d. Ma sœur est moins belle que ma mère.

e. Mon chien est plus bruyant que mon canard.

f. Ma tante est plus vieille que ma grand-mère.

g. Ma mère est aussi sportive que mon frère et moi.

6. Spot the missing words and write them in

Je m'appelle Jules. Dans ma famille trois personnes. Nous sommes sportifs, mais mes parents sont plus sportifs que moi. Nous sommes tous grands, mais je suis plus grand mes parents. Nous sommes tous peu gros, mais mon père est plus gros que mère et moi. Suis le plus mince de ma famille! Nous sommes tous travailleurs, mais mes parents sont plus travailleurs que moi. Je suis un paresseux.

7. Faulty translation: spot the translation errors and correct them

My name is Jean-François. In my family there are two persons: my father, my grandmother and me. We are all very slim, but I am slimmer than my parents. We are all funny, but my mother and I are more intelligent and hard-working than my father. We are all short, but my father and my cousin are taller than me. I am the silliest in the family.

8. Listen and complete the translation

Person	Description
1. My father is…	
2. My mother is…	
3. My older brother is…	
4. My younger brother is…	
5. My sister is…	
6. My uncle is…	
7. My grandma is…	
8. My best friend is….	
9. My girlfriend is…	
10. My dog is…	

9. Listen, spot and correct the errors

a. Ma mère est plus grand que moi.

b. Mon père est plus travailleur que mon.

c. Mon frère aîné suis plus fort que mon frère cadet.

d. Mon grand-père est plus vieille que ma grand-mère.

e. Je suis plus mince de mes parents.

f. Mes oncles sont beaucoup plus vieux que mes parents.

g. Mes grands-parents maternels sont plus vieux que mes grands-parents paternels.

h. Mes cousins est plus riches que vous.

 **THE LANGUAGE GYM**

25

10. Narrow listening: gapped translation

My name is Anthony and I am _____ years old. I am from Marseille, but I live in _____. In my family we are _____ persons: my parents, my two_____, Charles, Louis and me. Charles is_____, more handsome and _____ than Louis, but Louis is friendlier, more intelligent and more _____ than Charles. My _____ are called Fernand and Pauline. They are both very _____, but my father is _____ than my mother. Moreover, my mother is more patient and less stubborn than my father. I am as _____ as my father! I have a pet, a _____ called Cacahuète. My parents say Cacahuète is as _____ as me.

11. Listen and write down what order you hear each chunk of text

	My father is funnier than my mother.
	Gabrièle is prettier than Caroline.
	I am as generous as my mother.
1	**My name is Pauline.**
	Caroline is much nicer than Gabrièle.
	My father is less generous than my mother.
	I am twenty years old.
	However, my dog is as lazy as a sloth.
	I live with my parents and my two sisters, Gabrièle and Caroline.

12. Answer the questions below about Éric

a. How old is he?

b. Where does he live?

c. How many people are there in the family?

d. Paul is _____ and _____ than Jules.

e. Jules is _____ and _____ than Paul.

f. Why does he prefer his father?

g. He is as _____ as his mother.

h. Which of his pets is more talkative?

13. Listening slalom: follow the speaker from top to bottom and number the boxes accordingly

1	2	3	4
My mother is more (1)	My mother is as	My mother is less	My stepmother is
affectionate than my father,	**talkative than my father, (1)**	less hard-working than my mother,	hard-working as my father,
as sporty as	as lazy as	**as tall as (1)**	less generous than
my father	me	my older sister	**my younger sister (1)**
and less	and much more	**and more (1)**	and as
boring	**annoying (1)**	unfriendly	intelligent than
as my younger sister	her sisters	than my aunt	**than my brother (1)**

THE LANGUAGE GYM

UNIT 10 – SAYING WHAT IS IN MY SCHOOLBAG/CLASSROOM

1. Multiple choice quiz: what items do they have?

	a	b	c
1. Raphaël	a red pen	a red pencil	a red rubber
2. Alexandra	a modern computer	modern furniture	a modern classroom
3. Romain	three books	three pencil sharpeners	three felt tip pens
4. Gabrièle	a blue rubber	a blue textbook	a blue pen
5. Jean-Louis	some grey pencils	some blue pencils	some green pencils
6. Dylan	a black pencil case	a black textbook	a black rubber
7. Marie-Hélène	an orange pencil sharpener	an orange felt-tip pen	an orange rubber
8. Tristan	a red exercise book	a red pencil	a red ruler
9. Caroline	a white ruler	a white schoolbag	a white dictionary

2. Fill in the blanks

a. Dans ma _____, j'ai deux crayons.

b. Dans mon _____, il y a deux _____.

c. J'ai _____ d'un taille-crayon.

d. Mon _____ Paul n'_____ pas de gomme.

e. Je n'ai ni _____, ni _____-_____.

f. Dans mon _____, il y a une _____, deux _____ et trois _____.

g. Dans ma _____, il y a le _____ du professeur et vingt _____.

4. Spot the differences and correct your text

1. Dans mon sac il y a une trousse rouge, un livre d'anglais, un livre de géographie, deux cahiers bleus, un dictionnaire et une tablette.

2. Mon ami Charles a des feutres, des stylos, un taille-crayon, un stylo à plume et un tube de colle dans sa trousse. Il n'a pas d'agenda. Il n'a pas non plus de calculatrice.

3. Mon amie Caroline a une trousse verte. Dans sa trousse, elle a deux feutres, un agenda, une règle et un compas.

3. Listening for detail: tick which items the speaker does NOT have

Anne	a red pencil case
	two pens
	a gluestick
	a pencil sharpener
	a pencil
	six felt-tip pens
Sylvie	a green pencil case
	felt-tip pens
	two gluesticks
	three books
	a black pencil
	a white rubber
Véronique	a calculator
	a red ruler
	two books
	two pencils
	a rubber
	a fountain pen

5. Spot the missing words and write them in

Je m'appelle Raphaël. J'ai ans et je vis à Grenoble, en France. Dans ma famille, quatre personnes. Mon frère appelle Serge. Dans ma classe, il y a deux, et vingt-deux tables. Il y a aussi vingt-deux. Ma classe est jolie, mais mon professeur est très ennuyeux. Dans ma trousse, je n'ai pas de crayon, de stylo, ni de règle, ni de gomme. Je n'ai. J'ai de tout. À la maison, j'ai une souris, elle est très marrante elle s'appelle Pistache.

6. Faulty translation: spot and correct the errors

My name is Anthony. I am 14 years old and I live in Valence, in France. In my family, there are five persons. My father, my mother, my brother, my sister and me. We also have a very funny duck. In my classroom, there are many things. There is a window, a computer and thirty chairs. My classroom is very small. In my schoolbag, I have a blue pencil, a yellow compass, a new rubber and a white exercise book. My friend Marc has pens of all colours.

8. Listen, spot and correct the errors

a. J'ai besoin d'une stylo.

b. Mon ami Paul a huit feutres.

c. J'ai une sac blanche et deux gommes.

d. Ma classe petite, mais jolie.

e. Nous avons un animal en ma classe, un cochon d'Inde.

f. Dans ma trousse, j'ai deux compas.

g. Ma sœur besoin d'un ordinateur.

h. Mes cousins n'ont rien. Ils sont besoin de tout.

7. What do Louis and his friends need?

	Person	What they need…
1	I (Louis) need…	
2	My brother needs…	
3	Sylvie needs…	
4	Naomi needs…	
5	Patricia needs…	
6	Caroline needs…	
7	Raphaël needs…	
8	Michel needs…	
9	Rose needs…	
10	Thérèse needs…	

9. Narrow listening: gapped translation

My name is Simona and I am _____. I am _____ years old and I live in the _____ of Italy. In my family, there are _____ people. I have a white _____ and a black _____. In my _____ I have a lot of things. I have a green _____, a yellow felt-tip pen, a _____ ruler, a grey compass and a white and blue _____. My _____ is very big and _____. My best friend _____ Lucie. She has only got one _____ in her pencil case: a _____. In her house she has a pet. It is a _____, yellow and blue parrot that speaks and sings.

---

10. Listen and arrange the information in the same order as it occurs in the text

	I don't get along with my stepfather.
	In my family there are four people.
	I like my school.
1	**My name is Alexandra.**
	I love my mother.
	But in my classroom, there isn't a computer.
	I am twelve and I live in Angers.
	I have a brand-new school bag.
	Angers is in the west of France.
	…and I have many things inside.

11. Answer the questions below about Éric

a. Who is his favourite brother?

b. What does his father do for a living? And his mother?

c. What does he say about his school?

d. Why does he not like his classroom?

e. What 3 (different) things are there in his schoolbag?

f. What two things does he not have?

---

12. Listening slalom: follow the speaker from top to bottom and number the boxes accordingly

1	2	3	4
In my pencil case (1)	In his schoolbag	In my schoolbag	In her pencil case
there are	my sister has	**I only have (1)**	my brother has
a diary	many things	some pencils	**a pen (1)**
a few felt tip pens	**a pencil (1)**	there are two books	a pencil case
some exercise books	**a rubber (1)**	a calculator	three exercise books
a pencil sharpener (1)	a ruler	a red pencil case	a dictionary
and two pens	and a computer	and his tablet	**and scissors (1)**

THE LANGUAGE GYM

1. Listen and fill in the gaps

a. J'adore _____.

b. Raphaël aime beaucoup _____.

c. Paul n'aime pas du tout _____.

d. Alexandre adore _____.

e. Mon père adore _____ de fraises.

f. Ma mère déteste _____.

g. Mon frère adore _____.

h. Ma sœur raffole de _____ _____ épicé.

i. Je déteste _____.

2. Mystery words: guess the words, then listen and see how many you guessed right.

a. l'ea__

b. le m__e__

c. l'œ__f

d. la v__a__de

e. le p__ __l__ __

f. la p__ __m__

g. le p__ __n

h. le r__z

3. Listening for detail: tick which food items Martine and Serge usually eat for breakfast

Martine	Du beurre
	Des tartines
	Un jus de fruits
	De la confiture
	Un œuf
	Du fromage
	Un café au lait
Serge	Une saucisse
	Un œuf
	Du riz
	Un café
	Du pain avec du miel
	Un jus d'orange
	Une banane

4. Spot the differences and correct your text

a. J'adore les fruits, surtout les prunes.

b. Je déteste les légumes, surtout les champignons.

c. Je n'aime pas le poulet frit.

d. J'aime beaucoup les fruits de mer.

e. J'aime beaucoup les pâtes.

f. J'adore le jus de pomme.

g. La viande rouge est saine.

h. Le café est savoureux.

i. Les hamburgers sont sains.

j. Les légumes sont savoureux.

k. Les pommes sont croquantes.

l. Je n'aime pas beaucoup le lait.

 THE LANGUAGE GYM

5. Spot the missing words and write them in

Je m'appelle Fabrice. Qu'est-ce que tu manger? Moi, j'adore fruits de mer, donc j'aime les crevettes et les calamars, car ils sont délicieux. J'adore aussi le poisson, car savoureux et riche protéines. J'adore le saumon. J'aime le poulet rôti épicé. J'aime beaucoup les fruits, surtout les bananes. Je ne supporte pas les légumes parce qu'ils dégoûtants.

6. Faulty translation: spot the translation errors and correct them

My name is Phillipe. What do I enjoy eating? I love fruit, especially tomatoes. I drink them every day. My favourite vegetables are tomatoes and potatoes because they are rich in vitamins. I also like jam because it is delicious and fruit because it is tasty. I hate turkey and burgers. They are rich in protein, but they are not spicy.

8. Listen, spot and correct the spelling, grammar errors and wrong words

a. J'adore les légumes, car ils sont sains.

b. J'adorons les hamburgers.

c. Le poisson et la viande sont savoureuses.

d. J'aime beaucoup le jus d'orange.

e. Je mange trop de poisson, car c'est riche en protéines.

f. Je n'aime pas le viande, car c'est gras.

g. J'adore ce poulet rôti, car c'est savoureux.

h. J'apprécie beaucoup les calamars frits, même s'ils sont malsains.

7. Why do they like/dislike these foods?

People and what they like/dislike	Reasons why they like/dislike
1. I like fruit because	
2. My brother loves eggs	
3. Sylvie hates vegetables	
4. Naomi dislikes crêpes	
5. Pauline dislikes tomatoes	
6. Caroline loves oranges	
7. Raphaël loves Indian food	
8. Ahmed doesn't eat pork	
9. Rose dislikes sausages	
10. Jean likes fish	
11. Thérèse hates French fries	
12. Sophie hates carrots	

 **THE LANGUAGE GYM**

9. Narrow listening: gapped translation

Je m'appelle Julien. Qu'est-ce que j'aime manger? Je préfère la _____, surtout le _____. J'adore

ça, car c'est _____. J'aime _____ les hamburgers. J'adore aussi les _____.

Je les mange avec des _____. J'aime aussi beaucoup les fruits, car c'est _____. Je n'aime pas

les _____. Je déteste les tomates et les _____. Je n'aime pas non plus les

_____ et les _____. Ils sont _____. De plus, je ne supporte pas

les _____. Ils sont riches en protéines et vitamines, mais ils sont _____.

---

10. Listen and arrange the information in the same order as it occurs in the text

	She likes lamb and pork.
	She loves spinach and green beans.
	He also loves French fries.
1	**In my family there are four people.**
	My sister loves meat.
	My father's favourite food is roast chicken.
	We all like food and we eat a lot.
	Me, I like cakes and sweets.
	Vegetables are my mother's favourite food.
	I also love honey, because it's sweet and healthy.

11. Answer the questions below about Marie

a. How many people are there in Marie's family?

b. What do her parents love?

c. What does her mother hate?

d. What does her brother Raphaël love?

e. What does her brother Jean love?

f. What does Marie love?

g. What does she hate?

h. Why?

---

12. Listening slalom: follow the speaker from top to bottom and number the boxes accordingly

1	2	3	4
I love (1)	I hate	I can't stand	I love
chocolate	**meat (1)**	spinach	burgers
and cakes	sausages	**because it is (1)**	and tomatoes
or French fries	because they are sweet	because they are	**tasty (1)**
and delicious	disgusting.	**and rich in protein. (1)**	because they are
greasy	**I eat it with salad (1)**	I prefer	even if
they are a bit unhealthy.	and unhealthy.	**or French fries. (1)**	carrots.

UNIT 12 – TALKING ABOUT FOOD – LIKES & DISLIKES

1. Listen and fill in the gaps

a. En général, je mange un _____ pour le petit-déjeuner.

b. Parfois, je mange des _____ pour le petit-déjeuner.

c. …mais je mange rarement des _____.

d. Généralement, je mange du _____ avec du poulet ou de la _____ avec des légumes pour le déjeuner.

e. En général, je ne mange pas _____ pour le goûter.

f. De temps en temps, je prends du pain avec du _____ pour le goûter.

g. Normalement, je mange de la _____ pour le dîner.

h. Parfois, je mange des _____ ou du _____.

2. Mystery verbs: guess the words, then listen and see how many you got right

a. Je ne __ __ __g__ pas beaucoup pour le dîner.

b. Je __ __ __ __d__ du pain avec de la confiture.

c. Je __ __i__ beaucoup d'eau.

d. Je m__ __ __ __ de la viande avec de la salade.

e. J'a__ __ __ __ les fruits.

f. Je __ __t__ __ __ __ le poisson.

3. Listening for detail: tick which food items Serge usually eats for his various meals

Petit-déjeuner	Œufs Fruits Fromage Pain Miel
Déjeuner	Viande Riz Pâtes Poulet Soupe
Goûter	Confiture Gâteaux Lait Tartine Nutella
Dîner	Salade Fromage Viande Soupe Légumes
Boissons	Eau Café Jus de pomme Jus d'orange Café au lait Lait

4. Spot the differences and correct your text

Pour le petit-déjeuner, en général, je mange peu: une banane, deux ou trois poires, des tartines avec du miel, un jus d'orange et une tasse de thé au citron. J'aime le café sucré.

A midi, en général, je mange seulement du riz avec du poisson ou des légumes et je bois du jus de fruits. J'adore le poulet épicé car c'est délicieux et c'est riche en vitamines. Parfois, je mange des asperges. J'adore ça, car elles sont savoureuses et riches en vitamines.

Pour le dîner, je ne mange pas beaucoup. D'habitude, je mange du riz et de la viande avec des légumes, et pour le dessert je prends un yaourt ou je bois des gâteaux.

THE LANGUAGE GYM

5. Spot the missing words and write them in

Je m'appelle Fernand. En général, je ne mange pas pour le petit-déjeuner. Seulement un œuf et de thé. J'aime le thé sucré, beaucoup de sucre. Parfois, je bois du jus. A midi, je mange du poulet avec des légumes et je bois de l'eau. Je mange beaucoup de légumes car ils sont sains et délicieux. J'aimerais plus de crevettes, car j'adore ça! Après le collège, je prends deux tartines et je bois une tasse de thé. J'adore le miel délicieux. Pour le, je mange beaucoup. En général, je mange du riz, des fruits de mer avec des légumes et un ou deux gâteaux.

6. Faulty translation: spot the translation errors and correct them

My name is Robert. In general, I don't eat much for lunch. Only an apple and a lot of coffee.

At dinner, usually I eat fish with baked potatoes, and I drink mineral water. Sometimes, I eat roast turkey. I often eat burgers because they are tasty.

For dinner, I eat very much, generally rice or a salad.

7. Write in English what each person thinks about each food/drink

	Food	Opinion
1. Jean		

	Food/drink	Opinion
2. Dylan		

8. Listen, spot and correct the spelling and grammar errors

Je ne mange pas trop pour le petit-déjeuner, je prends seulement un œuf et une tasse de thé. J'aime la thé très sucré, avec beaucoup de lait. Parfois, je bois du d'ananas.

Midi, je mange du rôti poulet avec des légumes et je bois de minérale l'eau. Je mange beaucoup de légumes car ils est savoureux.

Après le collège, pour le dîner, je mange une tartine sans de la confiture.

Pour le dîner, je prends de la riz avec du poisson ou de la salade. Parfois, je mange une tarte aux fruits.

9. What do they have for lunch?

	What they eat and drink (three details)
1	
2	
3	
4	
5	
6	

 **THE LANGUAGE GYM**

10. Narrow listening: gapped translation

Usually, I don't eat _____ in the morning: a banana, one or two _____, bread with

_____, an _____ juice and cup of coffee _____ sugar. It's a very _____

breakfast, rich in vitamins and _____. At noon, I have _____ with _____ and

vegetables. I drink lemonade because it is _____ and delicious. For dinner, I have a _____ or

chicken soup with some _____. I love ice cream because it is _____.

---

11. Listen and arrange the information in the same order as it occurs in the text

	It is very healthy
	At noon I eat a lot
	I eat bread with honey or jam
1	**At breakfast I don't eat much**
	I eat chicken with vegetables
	I usually have fish or seafood
	At around 4pm I have my snack
	One or two eggs and a toast
	It is delicious!
	I also drink a coffee without sugar
	I have dinner around 7.30pm
	I drink 3 litres of water a day

---

12. Answer the questions below about Éric

1. What three things does he eat at breakfast?

a.

b.

c.

2. How does he describe his breakfast? (two adjectives)

a.

b.

3. What does he usually have for lunch?

a.

b.

c.

d.

4. At what time does he have dinner? _____

5. What does he have for dinner?

a.

b.

---

13. Listen to Paul talk about his family and fill in the grid

	Relationship to speaker	Starter	Main course	Dessert
Céline				
Mélanie				
Xavier				
Julien				

THE LANGUAGE GYM

1. Listen and fill in the gaps

a. À la maison, _____ un pull.

b. À la plage, je porte un _____.

c. Au gymnase, je porte un _____.

d. Je ne porte jamais de _____.

e. Quand il fait froid, je porte une _____.

f. Quand je sors en boîte, je porte une _____.

g. Mon frère porte toujours des _____ de sport.

h. Ma petite amie porte des _____ élégants.

2. Mystery words: guess the words, then listen and see how many you guessed right

a. Une é__ __ __ __ __ __ __

b. Une __ __ __m__ __ __

c. Une __u__ __

d. Un __a__ __ __ __ __

e. Un __ __ __l

f. Un __o__ __ __ __ __

g. Un __ __i__ __ __ __ de b__ __ __

3. Listening for detail: tick the clothes David wears

Ce que je porte quand il fait froid	Une écharpe
	Un pull
	Un manteau
	Des bottes
	Un maillot de bain
Ce que je porte quand je sors avec ma petite amie	Une chemise
	Une ceinture
	Un pantalon
	Des sandales
	Des chaussures élégantes
Ce que je porte quand je sors avec mes amis	Une veste de sport
	Une jupe
	Un chapeau
	Un gilet
	Des chaussures de sport
Ce que je porte quand je reste à la maison	Un pull
	Un tee-shirt
	Des pantoufles
	Un chapeau
	Un jean

4. Spot the differences and correct your text

Je m'appelle Alexandra. J'ai dix-sept ans. Je suis assez sportive et j'ai des vêtements de toutes les couleurs et de types différents.

Je préfère les vêtements de marque, mais pas trop bon marché. En général, à la maison je porte un survêtement ou un tee-shirt, un pantalon et des chaussures de sport ou des bottes.

Quand je vais au gymnase, je porte un manteau et des chaussures de sport blanches. J'ai six survêtements différents. Ils sont de marque, mais cela m'est égal.

Quand je sors avec mes amis, je porte une veste de costume, un jean et des chaussures de sport.

Quand je sors avec mon petit frère, je mets des robes élégantes et à la mode et mes chaussettes préférées. Elles sont aussi moches et confortables.

THE LANGUAGE GYM

5. Spot the missing words and write them in

Je m'appelle Jean-Paul. J'ai dix-huit. Je suis Cannes en France. Dans ma famille quatre personnes et je m'entends bien avec tout le monde. Nous avons animaux, un chien, un perroquet très bavard et un poisson. J'adore acheter des vêtements, surtout des chaussures et des tee-shirts de couleurs différents. Je n'ai pas de vêtements, mais j'aime beaucoup les vêtements. J'adore les vêtements de marque.

Quand il fait froid, je porte un manteau et un pantalon noir ou bleu. Parfois, je porte une de sport. Quand il fait chaud, je porte des tee-shirts manches, un jean des sandales. Ma nourriture, c'est la pizza. J'adore aussi et les pâtes. Je déteste légumes.

6. Faulty translation: correct the translation

I hate clothes. Especially sports clothes. I have many T-shirts. My favourite tracksuit is blue and red. I also have many sports shoes.

At home, I usually wear a T-shirt, new jeans and boots.

When I go out with my girlfriend, if it's hot, I wear a T-shirt and jeans. If it's cold, I wear a long coat and my favourite jeans.

8. Listen, spot and correct errors

Je m'appelle Serge. J'ai quinze ans. Quand je vais à collège, je porte une chemise bleue, un short bleu et des chaussures noires.

À la maison, en général, je porte un tee-shirt, une jean et pantoufles. J'ai trop de tee-shirts et de jeans.

Quand je vais au gymnase, je porte un tee-shirt sans manches, des shorts et des chaussures sport.

Quand je vais au centre-ville avec ma amis, je porte une veste, une chemise, un pantalon noir ou grise, et des chaussures noires.

7. Write in English the clothing item/accessory and description

	Noun	Adjective
1		
2		
3		
4		
5		
6		
7		
8		

9. What are they wearing?

	Four details each
1. Pauline	
2. Eva	
3. Sylvain	

THE LANGUAGE GYM

10. Narrow listening: gapped translation

Usually, in the winter at home I wear a _____, _____ trousers and _____. In the summer, on the other hand, I wear a _____, _____ and _____. I have a lot of _____ _____, but also some _____ clothes. I like _____ clothes, but it's very expensive, so I don't have _____. When I go out with my friends or with my _____ in the _____, I wear a _____ T-shirt, _____, trainers and _____. However, in the _____, I wear a coat, Levi's jeans and _____.

11. Listen and arrange the information in the same order as it occurs in the text

	I live in the south, in Provence
	At school I wear a navy blue shirt
1	**My name is Gabrièle**
	I have a yellow and blue parrot
	with jeans and trainers
	At home I wear a tracksuit
	and I live in France
	When I go out, I wear a pink T-shirt
	I have three brothers and a sister
	and black trousers

12. Listen to André's description of himself and his family and answer the questions below in English

1. Where is he from? (1)

2. How many siblings has he got? (1)

3. What are his favourite foods? (3)

4. Why? (1)

5. What does he usually wear? (3 details)

6. What are his favourite shoes? (2)

7. Who wears jeans and flip-flops every day? (1)

8. Who wears elegant clothes? (1)

13. Fill in the grid: what did they buy?

	Item bought	What for	Colour	Opinion	Price
Léa					
Anne					
Pierre					
Marie					

 **THE LANGUAGE GYM**

1. Complete with 'je joue', 'je fais' or 'je vais'

a. _____ aux échecs.

b. _____ de la musculation.

c. _____ aux cartes.

d. _____ de l'escalade.

e. _____ à la piscine.

f. _____ en boîte.

g. _____ chez un ami.

h. _____ avec mes amis.

2. Complete with the missing syllables

a. Je joue au te__ __ __ __.

b. Je fais de la rando__ __ __ __.

c. Je vais au centre spor__ __ __.

d. Je vais en boî__ __.

e. Je fais du vé__ __.

f. Je vais à la monta __ __ __.

g. Je joue au badmin__ __ __.

h. Je vais à la pla__ __.

i. Je vais au par__.

j. Je fais de la nata__ __ __ __.

3. Listening for detail: what activities does Aurélie do each day? Tick the correct one

Monday	▪ Cycling ▪ Chess ▪ Rock climbing
Tuesday	▪ Going to the mountain ▪ Swimming ▪ Going clubbing
Wednesday	▪ Going to the gym ▪ Playing basketball ▪ Playing tennis
Thursday	▪ Jogging ▪ Homework ▪ Horse riding
Friday	▪ Skiing ▪ Weights ▪ Chess
Saturday	▪ Hiking ▪ Weights ▪ Bike riding
Sunday	▪ Swimming ▪ Weights ▪ Fishing

4. Spot the intruder

Je m'appelle Thomas. Je suis un allemand. Je suis très sportif. Pendant mon temps libre, je fais souvent du sport. Mon sport préféré, c'est l'escalade libre. Je fais de l'escalade presque tous les jours. Quand il fait mauvais, en général, je reste chez moi et je joue aux échecs ou je joue aux cartes avec mon frère cadet. J'aime aussi beaucoup faire de la natation. Je fais de la natation presque tous les week-ends à la piscine près de chez moi maison.

5. Faulty translation: correct the translation

My name is Laura. I have red hair and I am very friendly and talkative. I am not very sporty. I prefer to read books, play chess, play cards and go shopping. When the weather is nice, I like going hiking and from time to time, I go to the park with my boyfriend. I rarely go to the gym. It is very boring in my opinion. I prefer to go jogging.

6. What are their favourite hobbies?

1. Ninon	
2. Serge	
3. Laure	
4. Jean-Paul	
5. Alexandre	
6. Lola	
7. Maurice	
8. Xavier	
9. Pascale	

7. Spot the differences and correct your text

Je m'appelle Clive. Je suis anglais. J'adore faire de l'escalade. J'y vais tous les jours avec mes amis. C'est mon sport préféré! Parfois, je fais de la musculation, du footing ou de la randonnée. Ce sont des sports passionnants. Je n'aime pas le tennis, ni le foot. Ce sont des sports ennuyeux à mon avis. Je déteste aussi faire de la natation. Je fais du vélo très souvent au vélodrome près de chez moi. Deux fois par semaine, je vais en boîte avec mon ami, Glenn. J'aime danser.

8. Split sentences: listen and match

1. Je fais du vélo	a. montagne
2. Je joue au	b. beau
3. Je vais chez	c. au parc
4. Je vais à la	d. l'équitation
5. Quand il fait	e. basket
6. Je déteste faire de	**f. tous les jours**
7. Je ne fais jamais	g. avec mon ami Paul
8. Je vais souvent	h. de la randonnée
9. Je vais à la pêche	i. un ami

9. Listen, spot and correct the grammar/spelling errors

a. Je joue des échecs.

b. Je vais à mon ami.

c. Je fais rarement de l'escalade.

d. Je joue presque jamais au foot.

e. Je vais le centre sportif.

f. Je vais à boîte.

g. Quand il beau, je fais du footing.

h. Je fais du vélo tous les jours.

10. Mystery words: guess the words then check

a. __s_a__ __d__

b. C__ __ __ __e__

c. N__ __ __ __ __o__ __

d. P__ __c

e. V_ l__

f. __k__

g. P__ __h__

h. T__ __ __s

i. L__ __ __ __ __

11. Spot the missing words and write them in

Je m'appelle Luna, et je suis italienne. J'adore faire vélo. Je fais du vélo avec amis. Mon sport préféré. J' fais tous les jours. De temps temps je fais de l'escalade, du footing, ou de la randonnée. Je n'aime pas du le tennis ni foot. Je déteste aussi de la natation. J'en très rarement car fatigant. Deux fois semaine, je vais boîte avec ma amie Julia. J'adore danser dans discothèque tous mes amis du collège.

12. Listen to Tristan talk about his friends and fill in the grid below in English

Name	Age	Description	Favourite food	Favourite clothes	Favourite sport	How often they practise sport
1. Christophe						
2. Anthony						
3. Arnaud						
4. Nico						
5. Gilles						

13. Narrow listening: gapped translation

My name is _____-_____ and I am _____ years old. I am _____ and Corsican. I am an inhabitant from _____, the 'isle of beauty'. I live here with my _____, my two _____ and my _____. My parents are very _____ and _____. My brothers are very _____ and my sister is funny and _____. What I like eating the most is _____ and _____. I also eat _____ very often. In my free time, I do a lot of _____. I play _____ at school _____. I often do _____ at the gym near my house. Three times a week, I go _____ and from time to time, I go to the _____ with my brothers. Besides sport, I also play _____ and I go to guitar _____ once a week. I love _____. Goodbye!

UNIT 15 – TALKING ABOUT WEATHER AND FREE TIME

1. Listen and fill in the gaps

a. Quand j'ai le _____, je joue aux échecs.

b. Quand le ciel est _____, je fais du vélo.

c. Quand il fait _____, je fais du footing.

d. Quand il fait _____, je vais à la plage.

e. Quand il _____, je vais au centre commercial.

f. Pendant la _____, je ne fais pas de sport.

g. Quand il _____, je ne fais pas de vélo.

h. Quand il y a de l'_____, je reste à la maison.

i. Quand il fait _____, je fais mes devoirs.

2. Mystery words: guess the words, then listen and see how many you guessed right

a. La __ __ __g__

b. Il fait __ __a__ __

c. Le __ e __ __

d. Le __ __l__ __ __

e. __ __g__ __ __

f. Quand il __ __ __ __t

g. Il y a des n__ __ __ __ __

h. Il fait __ __o__ __

3. Listening for detail: tick the activities these three people do at the weekend

Paul	Goes jogging
	Goes to the shopping centre
	Goes horse riding
	Does his homework
	Goes clubbing
Anne	Goes swimming
	Goes to the shopping centre
	Goes to the sports centre
	Plays on the computer
	Goes to restaurant
Caroline	Goes jogging
	Goes to the shopping centre
	Goes horse riding
	Plays chess
	Goes to her friend's house

4. Fill in the blanks with the appropriate words

Qu'est-ce que je fais pendant mon temps libre? Beaucoup de choses. Quand il fait beau, je vais toujours au _____. J'aime _____, donc je fais du _____, seul ou avec mon _____. Mon chien aime aussi courir. Par ailleurs, j'_____ faire de l'escalade et de la _____. De temps en temps, quand il ne _____ pas, je fais de la randonnée dans le bois près de chez moi. J'habite à la _____. Quand le ciel est _____ et qu'il fait _____, je vais à la _____. J'adore la _____ et bronzer au _____. Quand il fait _____, surtout quand il _____, je reste à la maison. Je surfe sur _____, je fais mes devoirs, je joue aux _____ avec mon frère aîné ou je lis un _____. J'adore passer du temps en _____.

5. Spot the missing words and write them in

Je m'appelle Thomas. Je suis Suisse. J'ai dix-huit. Quand il chaud et que le ciel est dégagé, je vais la piscine et

je de la natation. Je aussi parfois à la pêche avec père sur bateau. C'est peu ennuyeux, mais cela plaît. Le, je vais

en boîte avec mes amis. Quand je vais boîte, en général, je porte tee-shirt et un jean. Mon amie appelle Sophie.

Elle est sympathique intelligente. Il fait mauvais et qu'il pleut, reste toujours à la maison et fait devoirs.

6. Faulty translation: correct the translation

In my free time, I do lots of sport. First of all, I like to sing and to play the guitar. Moreover, I like to buy shirts, jackets and sports clothes. I love to go shopping when it is rainy. When the weather is hot, I like to go to the beach or hiking in the woods. When it is nice, I prefer to go to the beach or the pool to swim. When it is foggy, I go windsurfing or sailing. In the winter, when it rains, I quite like to go to the shopping centre with my family. I love surfing.

8. Listen, spot and correct the spelling and grammar errors

Je m'appelle Patrice. Je suis à Biarritz, mais je vis à Nice, dans la sud-est de la Provence. Je suis grand et musclé. Je vis avec mon parents et mon frère cadet, Georges. Je m'entends très bien avec mes grands-parents. Nous passons peu de temps ensemble. J'aime beaucoup jouer aux échecs avec mon père et à la cartes avec ma mère. Je passe aussi beaucoup de temps avec ma sœur. Nous jouons du sport ensemble: du footing, de la natation et de la équitation. Le week-end, nous allons à boîte ensemble.

7. Write in English what each person thinks about different types of weather

	Opinion	Weather	Activity
1	Loves	Hot	Beach
2			
3			
4			
5			
6			
7			
8			

9. Sentence puzzle: rewrite the sentence in the correct order, then listen to check your answers

a. il fait quand froid je reste la maison à

b. commercial je vais faire quand il fait magasins mauvais les au centre

c. jouons aux quand il pleut échecs mon père et moi

d. plage quand il chaud va on à la fait

e. allons promenade il fait parc beau nous faire une dans le quand

f. ski neige quand nous du à la montagne il faisons

g. quand dégagé je fais avec chien le ciel est du footing mon

10. Listen and arrange the text in the correct order

	It's a boring job
	I am a student
	When it's hot, I go to the beach
1	**I live in Dakar, in Sénégal**
	In the summer, I work in a shop
	When it's windy
	I love sport
	I am tall and muscular
	I love to swim
	I am funny and friendly
	I also enjoy scuba diving
	I go sailing

11. Listen to Denise and answer the questions below in English

1. Which city is she from? In which country is this located?

2. Where does she live?

3. What is the weather like?

4. What does she do when the weather is bad? (three details)

5. What does she do when the weather is nice? (three details)

12. Listen to Anne talk about her family and then fill in the grid

	I (Anne)	My mother	My father	My sister
Personality				
Physique				
Favourite clothes				
What they do in good weather				
What they do in bad weather				
What they do when it is hot				

1. Listen and fill in the gaps

1. Il est six heures et __ __ __ __ __.

2. Il est __ __ __ heure.

3. Il est six heures et __ __ __ __ __.

4. Je me lève vers __ __ __ heures.

5. Je sors de chez moi à __ __ __ __ heures et demie.

6. Je vais au collège à huit heures __ __ __ __ __ le quart.

7. Je déjeune à __ __ __ __.

8. Je fais mes devoirs __ __ __ __ cinq heures.

9. Je me couche vers neuf __ __ __ __ __ __.

2. Multiple choice quiz: daily routine times

	a	b	c
1	6:00 am	7:00 am	9:00 am
2	10:00 am	10:05 am	10:10 am
3	2:45 pm	3:45 pm	2:15 pm
4	6:15 pm	5:45 pm	6:05 pm
5	11:05 am	10:55 am	10:25 am
6	2:30 pm	2:15 pm	2:20 pm
7	3:15 pm	2:45 pm	2:35 pm
8	12 pm	12 am	1 pm
9	7:20 am	7:10 am	7:50 am
10	8:15 am	7:45 am	2:35 am

3. Which of the following times do you hear in the text? Tick the ones you hear

4:00	7:30
6:00	8:05
6:15	8:25
6:20	12:00
7:20	12:10

4. Write out the times below, then listen to check if they are correct

1. 8:15 = huit heures et quart

2. 7:45 =

3. 9:20 =

4. 6:40 =

5. 11:30 =

6. 9:25 =

7. 10:35 =

8. Midnight =

9. Midday =

5. Spot the differences and correct your text

Je m'appelle Renaud. Je suis français. Je me réveille toujours vers six heures et demie. Ensuite, je me douche et je m'habille après. Je ne mange pas énormément le matin, mais mon frère Valentin mange des céréales dans la salle à manger avec ma mère. Je vais au collège en vélo vers sept heures et quart. Je rentre à la maison vers quatre heures et quart et ensuite je me détends un peu. En général, je joue de la musique dans le salon. Après, je surfe sur internet, je regarde une série sur Netflix ou des vidéos sur TikTok dans ma salle de jeux. Ensuite, à huit heures, je prépare le repas avec ma mère dans la cuisine. J'adore préparer des biscuits car ils sont dégoûtants. Je me couche tard, vers onze heures et demie.

6. Spot the missing words and write them in

Je m'appelle Fabien. Je suis Gibraltar. J'ai un chien la maison. Là où j'habite, il y a de singes. Je lève toujours tôt, à six heures quart. Ensuite, je vais au gymnase et je du sport. Je me douche je rentre à la maison. Mon frère Joël très paresseux. Il se lève à sept heures. Joël joue pas au foot et il ne fait jamais de sport. Ainsi, il est gros. Le soir, des bandes dessinées dans ma chambre ou j'écoute de la musique. La semaine, quand je rentre à la maison, je fais devoirs dans le salon avec ma mère. J'aime ma mère car est très intelligente et aide toujours. Finalement, je me couche à neuf heures dans chambre.

7. Faulty translation: correct the translation

My name is Akiko, I am Chinese. My daily routine is quite simple. In general, I get up very early, at 5:00. I go jogging and then I shower. Afterwards, I have breakfast with my mother around 7:15. Normally, I eat an egg or two and I have some cereals. Around 8:00 I leave my house and I go to school by bus. I come back home from school at around 3:30. Then, I rest a bit. In general, I watch a tv series and I chat with my friends on social media. From 6:00 to 8:00, I do my homework. I love doing my homework! Then, at around 8:15, I have dinner with my family. I don't eat a lot. Only a salad and some meat or fish. Afterwards, I play on my Playstation until 12:00. Finally, I go to bed.

8. Listen and note down in English what Caroline does at each time

Time	Activity
6:30	
7:15	
8:00	
9:15	
3:30	
3:45	
6:30	
10:00	
11.00	

9. Listen, spot and correct the errors

Je m'appelle Alex. Je suis de Belle-Île-en-Mer. J'ai deux chevals chez moi. Je ne lève toujours tôt, à six heures à quart. Ensuite, je vais au centre sportif et je joue du badminton. Je me couche quand je rentre à la maison, mais mon frère Joël a très paresseux et ne te douche jamais. Il se lève à sept heures. Joël ne joue jamais le foot, et ne fait jamais de sport. Par conséquent, il va très gros. Dans la semaine, quand je rentre chez moi, je fais mon devoirs dans le salon avec ma mère. J'aime ma mère, car elle est très intelligente et me aide toujours. Finalement, je me couche à neuf heures.

10. Listening slalom: follow the speaker and number the boxes accordingly

1. Myriam	2. René	3. Tristan	4. Sophie
Je me réveille. (1)	Je me lève.	Je me douche.	Je sors du collège.
Ensuite, je vais au gymnase.	Ensuite, je me lève. (1)	Ensuite, je prends mon petit-déjeuner.	Ensuite, je m'habille.
Après, je rentre à la maison,	Après, je m'habille,	Après, je prépare mon sac,	Après, je me douche, (1)
et ensuite, je sors de chez moi. (1)	et ensuite, je sors de chez moi.	et ensuite, je me peigne.	et ensuite, je me repose un peu.
Finalement, je fais mes devoirs.	Finalement, je m'habille.	Finalement, mon père me conduit au collège en voiture. (1)	Finalement je vais au collège.

11. Narrow listening: gapped translation

My name is Pierre. I am _____. I am from _____. My daily routine is very _____. In general, I get up _____, at around five thirty. Then I shower and _____ my uniform. _____, I have breakfast with my brothers. Then, I _____ and prepare my _____. At around _____ past seven, I leave home and go to school. I _____ home at around four. After this, I rest _____. Generally, I read my _____ magazines. From six to _____ I do my homework. Then, at eight, I have _____. I don't eat _____. Afterwards, I read a _____ or I surf on the _____. Finally, I _____ at 10:35.

12. Fill in the grid: what do the different people do?

	Me (Valérie)	My mother	My father	My sister
At 7:30				
At 8:15				
At 12:00				
From 3:00 to 4:00				
From 6:00 to 8:00				
From 8:30 to 11:00				

THE LANGUAGE GYM

UNIT 17 – DESCRIBING MY HOUSE

1. Multiple choice quiz

	a	b	c
1. J'habite	dans une ferme	dans un appartement	dans une maison
2. Mes grands-parents habitent	à la montagne	dans la banlieue	en centre-ville
3. Mes cousins habitent	à la campagne	dans un quartier chic	en centre-ville
4. Mon meilleur ami habite	près de la plage	en centre-ville	sur la côte
5. Ma petite amie habite	au bord de la mer	à la campagne	à la montagne
6. Mon oncle et ma tante habitent	dans une maison	dans une vieille maison	dans un manoir

2. Listening slalom: follow the speaker from top to bottom and number the boxes accordingly

1	2	3	4
J'habite dans une grande (1)	J'habite dans un	J'habite dans un petit	Dans ma maison
vieil appartement,	**et jolie maison (1)**	il y a six	chalet
assez chaleureux	pièces.	**dans la banlieue (1)**	mais il est près de
Ma pièce	la côte.	à la montagne.	**de Paris. (1)**
Mon endroit	préférée	**J'adore ma maison, (1)**	Ma pièce
préférée est	**car elle est (1)**	préféré, c'est	est
la terrasse.	le salon.	**neuve et moderne. (1)**	ma chambre.

3. Spot the differences and correct your text

Je m'appelle Michel et j'étais de Nernier, près de Genève. J'ai quinze ans. J'ai les cheveux châtains et les yeux bleus. Physiquement, je suis grand et gros. De caractère, je suis timide et assez calme. Je m'entends bien avec ma famille, car ils sont tous généreux. Ma nourriture préférée, ce sont les fruits de mer. J'en mange tous les jours. Je suis très sportif, et pendant mon temps libre, j'aime faire du foot, jouer au tennis, aller au cinéma et faire de l'équitation. En général, je me douche très tôt, vers six heures et je me couche à midi. J'habite dans une petite et jolie maison dans le centre de Genève, près du stade. J'adore ma maison. Ma pièce préférée est le salon, car c'est très lumineux et c'est très bien agencé.

4. Spot the missing words and write them in

Je m'appelle Fabrizio. Je viens Italie. J'habite dans grande et jolie maison sur la côte. Chez moi, dix pièces et ma pièce favorite, la cuisine. J'aime cuisiner dans la avec ma mère. Tous les jours, je lève, je me douche dans la salle et ensuite, je habille dans ma chambre. Je joue souvent mon ordinateur le salon. Mon ami Pablo habite dans une maison à la montagne. C'est une maison très vieille, très chaleureuse. Pablo est marrant et travailleur. Il n'aime pas maison, car elle est petite.

5. Faulty translation: correct the translation

My name is Romain, I am in Biarritz, in the Basque country. My house is in the centre of the city and I live far from the coast. At home, I speak Basque and French. Basque is a very beautiful and very new language. I live in a big apartment; it is old and beautiful. The rooms are very tiny. I have a huge garden with a small table. My horse lives in the garden. Its name is Papinou. My favourite thing at home is the kitchen because I love eating. I also like to relax in my living room. I always watch movies and series on Netflix. I also do my sport there.

6. Fill in the grid

	Description of house	Favourite part of the house
1		
2		
3		
4		
5		
6		
7		
8		

7. Gapped sentences: fill in the gaps

a. J'habite dans une grande et _____ maison.

b. Ma maison est dans la _____ de Valence.

c. J'ai aussi une maison à la _____.

d. Mon meilleur ami habite dans un appartement très _____ en _____-_____.

e. Ma petite amie habite dans un _____ appartement dans un quartier _____ sur la _____.

f. Mes grands-parents vivent à la _____.

g. Mon oncle favori, Paul, habite dans un _____ dans le centre-ville de Lyon.

8. Listen, spot and correct the spelling and grammar errors

Je m'appelle Penny. Je suis anglais et je vis dans une vieille mansion à la campagne, dans Italie. J'adore ma maison! Chez mon, il y a 5 pièces, mais ma pièce préfére, c'est le salon. Tous des jours, après la collège j'aime se reposer dans le salon et regarder le télé avec ma sœur. Je n'aime pas la salle des bain, car parfois il y a des souris! Nous avons une salle de bain assez grande où mon frère et moi joue à la Playstation.

9. Complete in English with the correct details

	Caroline	Philippe	Jean-Marc
Town			
Description of house (2 details)			
Location of house			
Favourite room			
Another room they like			
Room they hate			

10. Narrow listening: gapped translation

My house is very _____ and warm. It is situated on the _____ of Cannes, a city in the south of France, on the _____, five minutes away from the Midi _____. I live in a _____ _____. In my house there are six rooms: a kitchen, a toilet, a living room, and three _____. My favourite room is the _____ because it is _____, well-furnished and beautiful. I also like my bedroom because I have my Playstation and my _____. I like to _____ and do my homework in my bedroom. I hate the _____ because it is too _____ and old and on top of that, it smells very _____.

11. Answer the questions in English

1. How old is Oscar?

2. Where is he from?

3. Where does he live?

4. What does he look like? (3 details)

5. What is his character like? (3 details)

6. What are his favourite clothes? (2 details)

7. What's his favourite food? (2 details)

8. At what time does he wake up?

9. After school he goes for a walk with _____ and then he _____.

10. Does he live in a house or in a flat?

11. What is his house/flat like? (2 details)

12. What is his favourite room?

13. What is the room he hates the most?

14. What does he say about his bedroom? (2 details)

1. Mosaic listening: Follow the speaker from <u>left</u> to <u>right</u> → and number accordingly

1	**Vers sept heures (1)**	je prépare le repas	et je joue sur mon ordinateur	dans ma chambre
2	En général	**je prends mon petit-déjeuner (1)**	des films	dans la salle de jeux
3	Quand j'ai le temps	j'écoute de la musique et	**dans la cuisine (1)**	dans le salon
4	Souvent	j'aide	avec ma mère	**avec mes frères (1)**
5	Parfois	je surfe sur internet	je fais mes devoirs	dans le jardin
6	Tous les week-ends	je regarde	mon père	dans la cuisine

2. Listen and fill in the gaps

a. Souvent, je _____ avec ma mère dans la cuisine.

b. De temps en temps, je joue à la Playstation dans la salle de _____.

c. Deux fois par semaine, je _____ du vélo.

d. Souvent, je prépare le repas dans la _____.

e. Je fais toujours mes devoirs dans le _____.

f. En général, je me douche dans la _____ de bain de mes parents.

g. Quand il fait beau, je _____ des magazines dans le jardin.

h. Je ne _____ jamais la télé dans le salon avec mes parents.

3. Break the flow

a. Jeneregardejamaislatélédanslesalonavecmesparents.

b. Engénéraljerangemonvélodanslegarage.

c. TouslesjoursjepostedesphotossurInstagram.

d. Uneoudeuxfoisparsemainejeprépparelerepasdanslacuisine.

e. Jeneprendsjamaismonpetit-déjeuneravecmesfrèresdanslasalleàmanger.

f. Engénéralaprèslecollègejeregardelatélédansmachambre.

4. Faulty translation: what, how often, where? Listen and correct the errors

	What do they do?	How often?	Where?
1	Chats with his mother	Sometimes	In the kitchen
2	Helps father	Once a week	In the garage
3	Watches TV	Every day	In the living room
4	Does homework	Five times a week	In the living room
5	Goes on the internet	Often	In his parents' room
6	Has dinner	Every day	In the dining room
7	Prepares food	Never	In the kitchen
8	Rides his bike	From time to time	In the living room

5. Likely or Unlikely? Write "L" or "U" for each sentence you hear and then explain why

1		
2		
3		
4		
5		
6		
7		
8		

6. List the activities in the correct order in which Philippe does them
(there is a small amount of extra information included in the recording)

	I do my homework
	I go on the internet
	I listen to music
1	**I have breakfast**
	I read my favourite magazines
	I leave the house
	I watch a movie
	I brush my teeth
	I rest in my bed

7. Listen to the verbs and add them in where appropriate

a. Je _____ avec ma mère.

b. Je _____ sur internet.

c. Je _____ le repas.

d. Je _____ mes devoirs.

e. Je _____ les dents.

f. Je _____ des céréales.

g. Je _____ des photos sur Instagram.

h. Je _____ des films.

8. Narrow listening: gapped translation

_____ _____, I get up at five in the morning. Then I _____ and I have breakfast in the

_____. After that, I brush my teeth and I _____ my _____. Then, I _____ _____ and

I go to school at _____. Normally, I go by _____. When I _____ _____, I chat on Skype

with my family in Australia and I go on the internet in my _____. Then, I _____ in the

garden with my two _____. Sometimes, I watch _____ and I post photos on Instagram in my

brother's _____. Usually, I have dinner at around _____. After dinner, I _____ _____

and then I shower. Finally, I read my favourite _____ and I go to bed at _____.

9. Sentence puzzle: listen and rewrite correctly

1. tôt six heures Je me toujours, vers moins dix réveille.

2. petit-déjeuner, je un œuf mange avec de la seulement et tartines confiture Pour le deux.

3. chez moi à sept heures moins collège Je sors de le quart et en vélo je vais au.

4. qui s'appelle Joël J'ai très paresseux un antipathique frère et il est et.

5. chiens fais du vélo dans le je avec mes deux Tous les jours, jardin.

6. regarde après le dîner, je En général, la télé ou seul avec mes parents dans le salon.

10. Answer the questions about Marie
(EXTENSION: write down some extra details that you hear)

1. At what time does she always get up during the week?

2. How does she go to school?

3. What is her favourite school subject?

4. What two sports does she do after school?

5. Where does she normally chat with her mother?

6. In which room does she do her homework?

7. What does she never do during dinner?

8. What three things does she do after dinner?

9. What two things does she do before going to bed?

10. At what time does she go to bed?

1. Listen and fill in the gaps

1. Cet été, je _____ aller en vacances en Corse.

2. Je vais voyager en _____.

3. Nous allons _____ une semaine là-bas.

4. Ce _____ divertissant.

5. Je vais _____ dans un hôtel de luxe.

6. Je vais _____.

7. Nous allons faire les _____.

8. J'aimerais faire de la _____.

9. Nous aimerions _____ du sport.

2. Spot the differences and correct your text

a. Cet hiver, je vais aller en vacances au Maroc.

b. Je vais passer trois jours là-bas.

c. Je vais y aller avec mon petit ami.

d. Nous allons rester dans un hôtel de luxe .

e. Je vais faire du piano.

f. Mon père va acheter des chaussures.

g. Nous allons aller à la piscine.

h. Je vais me détendre au soleil.

i. J'aimerais faire de la natation.

j. Nous aimerions lire des magazines.

3. Listen and tick the correct details

Paul	va aller au Japon va voyager en bateau va rester dans un hôtel de luxe va manger beaucoup de sushis va aller en boîte
Anne	va aller en Italie va voyager en train va rester dans un camping va faire du tourisme va manger beaucoup de pâtes
Carole	va aller en France va voyager en vélo va rester dans une auberge de jeunesse va aller à la plage va visiter des sites historiques
Céline	va aller en Grèce va voyager en avion et en bateau va faire de la plongée va faire du tourisme va manger beaucoup de salades niçoises

4. Write in the missing words

Cet été, je vais aller en vacances _____ Rome, _____ Italie. Je _____ voyager en avion. Nous allons passer une semaine _____. Nous allons _____ dans un hôtel _____ luxe. _____ vais aller en boîte. Mes sœurs vont aller faire _____ magasins et mes parents vont _____ acheter des souvenirs et faire du tourisme car _____ beaucoup de sites historiques _____.

5. Guess what comes next then listen to see how many you guessed right

a. Je vais aller en vacances en _____.

b. Je vais passer _____ jours là-bas.

c. Je vais rester dans un _____.

d. Le matin, je vais aller _____.

e. L'après-midi, je vais faire du _____.

f. Le soir, je vais aller _____.

6. Multiple choice quiz

	a	b	c
1	He is Swiss	He is Swedish	He is Russian
2	He is travelling by train	He is travelling by plane	He is travelling by boat
3	He is travelling alone	He is travelling with his friend	He is travelling with his family
4	He is going to stay in a cheap hotel	He is going to stay in a three-star hotel	He is going to stay in a luxury hotel
5	He is going to stay there for 2 weeks	He is going to stay there for 3 weeks	He is going to stay there for 10 days
6	He is going to scuba dive	He is going to go clubbing	He is going to eat and sleep
7	He is also going to go sightseeing	He is also going to go shopping	He is also going to sunbathe
8	It will be fun	It will be great	It will be expensive

7. Faulty translation: spot the translation errors and correct them

This winter, I am going to go on holiday to Reunion Island. I am going to travel by train. I am going to go there with my brother. We are going to spend ten weeks there. We are going to stay in a good hotel in Saint-Denis, the capital of Reunion Island. It is a very loud place with a lively nightlife. There are lots of museums and our hotel is far from the sea. Every day, I am going to go to the beach. In the morning, I am going to swim and surf. I am also going to rest. In the afternoon, we are going to go shopping. My parents are going to buy clothes and my sister is going to buy lots of books, as always. For dinner, we will go to French restaurants. We will eat a lot of meat and pasta.

8. Listen, spot and correct the spelling and grammar errors

Ce été, je vais aller à vacances avec avion en Allemagne. Je vais passe deux semaine là-bas. Je vais y aller avec toute mon famille. Nous allons rest dans un hotel de luxury avec une piscine près de la river. Le matin, nous allons aller à la peach. L'après-midi, nous allons faire less magasins et faire du tourisme. Vers huit heures, nos allons dîner dans un restaurante local pour manger des plats typicals. Le soir, ma sœur et moi avons aller en boîte. J'aime aussi visiter Berlin. Ce serra génial!

9. Complete with the correct details in English

Holiday destination	
Means of transport	
Duration	
Who with	
Accommodation	
Activities	

THE LANGUAGE GYM

10. Listen and arrange the information in the same order as it occurs in the text

1	My name is Gabrièle
	We are going to stay there nine days
	This summer I am going to go on Holiday to Corsica
	The hotel is near the beach
	We are going to sunbathe
	We are going to travel by boat
	We are going to go to the beach every day
	We are going to stay in a four-star hotel
	We are going back home on 13th July
	We are going to scuba dive
	I am going to go with my best friends
	At night we are going to go clubbing

11. Listen to Charles and answer the questions below in English

1. In which part of France is he going on holiday?

2. When does his holiday begin?

3. How long for?

4. How is he travelling?

5. Who with?

6. Who are they staying with?

7. In which part of town are they going to stay?

8. What activities are they going to do? (4 details)

a.

b.

c.

d.

12. Fill in the grid in English

	Caroline	Benjamin	Sophie	Mathieu
Destination				
Who with				
Departure date				
How long for				
Accommodation				
Location				
Activities				

9 783949 651083